ON THE ROAD TO NOWHERE

A History of Greer, Arizona
1879-1979

Karen Miller Applewhite

ON THE ROAD TO NOWHERE
A History of Greer, Arizona
1879-1979

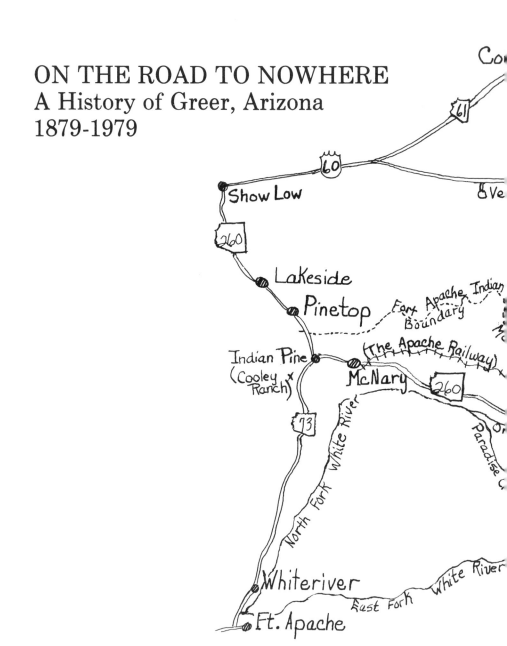

Written and Illustrated by
KAREN MILLER APPLEWHITE

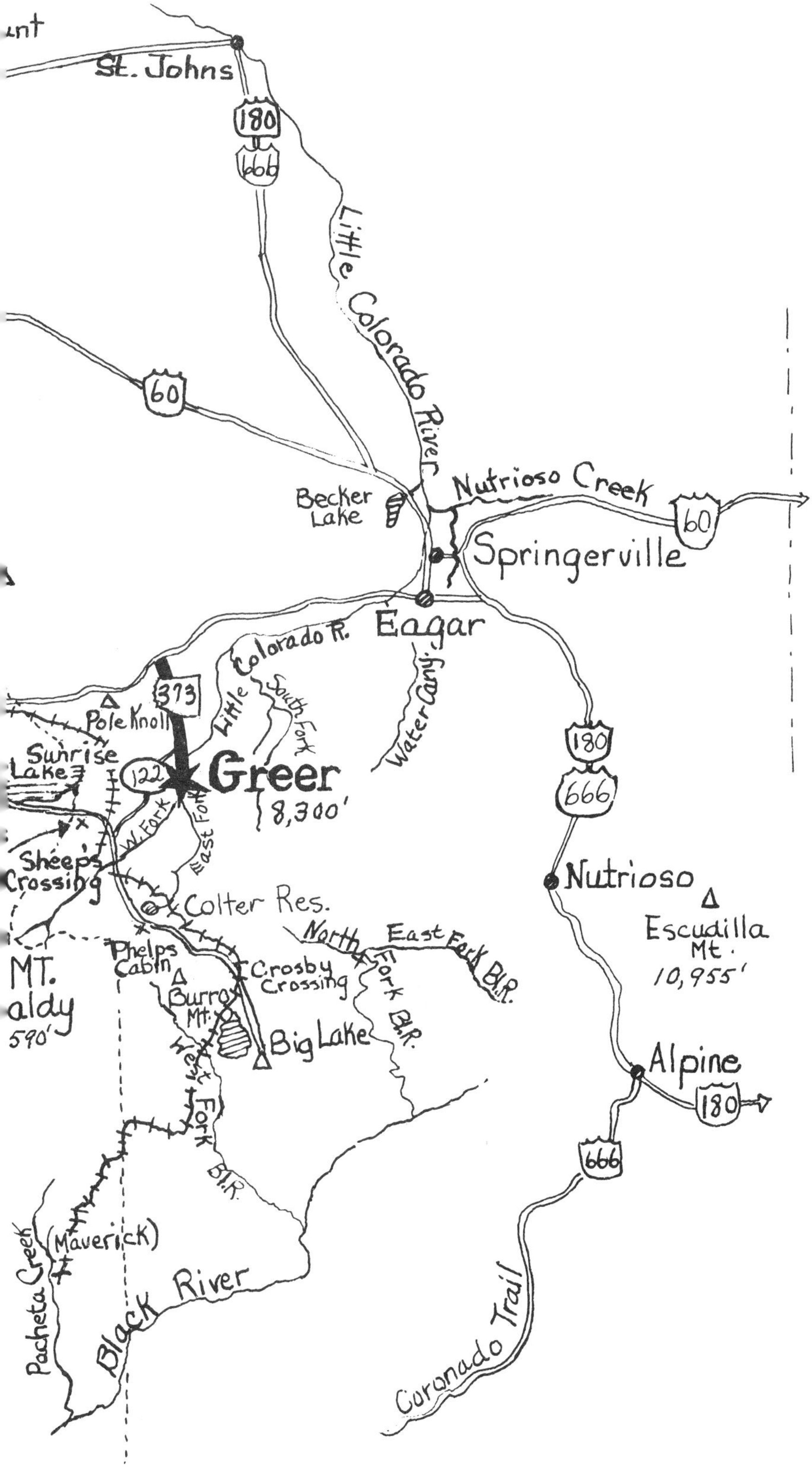

St. Johns
180
666
Little Colorado River
60
Becker Lake
Nutrioso Creek
60
Springerville
Eagar
Little Colorado R.
South Fork
Water Cany.
373
Pole Knoll
Sunrise Lake
122
Greer
8,300'
W. Fork
East Fork
Sheeps Crossing
Colter Res.
Phelps Cabin
Crosby Crossing
North Fork B.R.
East Fork B.R.
MT.
aldy
590'
Burro Mt.
Big Lake
West Fork B.R.
180
666
Nutrioso
Escudilla Mt.
10,955'
Alpine
180
666
(Maverick)
Pacheta Creek
Black River
Coronado Trail

Library of Congress Catalogue Card Number 79-54966
International Standard Book Number: 0-9603472-0-8

Published by
Karen Miller Applewhite
5942 East Sage Drive
Scottsdale, Arizona 85253

Printed in the United States of America
First Edition, Second Printing

Contents

He veils the sky in clouds
and prepares rain for the earth;
he clothes the hills with grass
and green plants for the use of man.
He gives the cattle their food
and the young ravens all that they gather.

. . . .

For he has put new bars in your gates;
he has blessed your children within them.
He has brought peace to your realm
and given you fine wheat in plenty.
He sends his command to the ends of the earth,
and his word runs swiftly.
He showers down snow, white as wool,
and sprinkles hoar-frost thick as ashes;
crystals of ice he scatters like bread-crumbs;
he sends the cold, and the water stands frozen,
he utters his word, and the ice is melted;
he blows with his wind and the waters flow.

(Psalm 147: 8-9, 13-18, NEB)

This Book is Dedicated
To my mother, Joella Coffin Miller,
who shared with me her
love of the land;
and
To my father, John E. "Brick" Miller,
who shared with me his
love of language.

Preface

Doctor, Lawyer, Merchant, Chief—
Rich Man, Poor Man, Beggar Man, Thief

Greer is a dent on Arizona's topography—A "where's that?" kind of place, sometimes forgotten, or deemed too small to be spotted on maps dealing with major towns and cities.

So why a "history"? Of what significance or interest is such a thing to anyone except to an almost extinct breed called "natives," their descendants; and briefly, to the detached tourist who comes for an interlude to cool off, catch his fish, let the kids catch a little local color, the wife ensconce herself on a webbed lawn chair with a good paperback and nibbles, then returns to the torrid tempo of civilization. No battles have been fought here; no famous personalities forged; no notorious scoundrels nor registered saints materialized (though minor varieties are known in both categories); no pace-setting structures built; no inventions recorded; no dynasties founded nor destroyed; no thriving industries nor large-scale developments ever undertaken—The whole story could be "done" on one page.

Other than a few diaries, recorded instruments, birth and death records, deeds, business statistics, etc., there are few hard facts. About all one has to go on is the other person's word and he or she may be "too young, too old, too dumb, too deaf, too blind, too mean, too pigheaded, too senile, too new-here, too sentimental, too drunk, too sober, too vague, too detailed, too biased, too detached to get it right!" Human memory edits according to its own book of etiquette. What is one man's "fact" is to another, "fancy."

Tracking down the story means people remembering their history —in voices that catch; that crackle with pride; that tighten with bitterness, unspoken hurts; that melt in nostalgia; that sometimes hesitate, carefully choosing words to launder the unmentionables. But it also involves pouring out their experiences spontaneously, with authenticity, tears and laughter—understated stories of people willing to take on often difficult lives with realism and courage.

Into this small settlement wandered people with all the human qualities and from every station in life: "Doctor, lawyer, merchant, chief; rich man, poor man, beggar man, thief"—each with his or her own history to create, tale to tell, part to play.

Greer, Arizona is a settlement on a small scale where lives are reduced to simpler terms—a microcosm, cross-section representative of small-town America, from which we all come at some level and which still generates a stabilizing force for many.

Arthur E. Leeds who for many years had a store, filling station, and sawmill operation in Greer has been a weekend, "anytime-I-can-find artist" for as long as he can remember. In speaking of how he looks at things:

> I learned from childhood on up, when you see something you're looking at and have any time at all, see what makes it look like it is, thick or thin, or moving from you—depth and feel. Feel of a leaf and see how it's made. And I got in that habit when fishing, hunting, or tracking. I'd stop long enough to see pine needles, oak leaves to see what made them look like they did.

A metaphor—One needs to go up to find out why something is the way it is. That's true not only for an artist but for anyone who cares about a thing, a person, a period. He or she takes time to go into something in depth and find out what it is about those things, people, places that make them the way they are, the way they were. The greater the understanding, the more appreciation one has not only for the past but for the present. It places one on a continuum—not simply cut loose, drifting alone on the surface of human history. "Insignificance" may depend on the eye that looks, the ear that hears, the heart that perceives the possibilities for depth. In knowing a period, a people, there is more to be learned than simply "facts."

Much of this book is based on interviews with a variety of people on their experiences during Greer's earlier days as well as their comments on its present and projections for its future. Some of these conversations were taped and will eventually be made available to the public through the Round Valley Historical Society, Springerville, Arizona. Those interviewed, with graciousness and enthusiasm, have provided facts and the flavor to make them palatable and lively.

Secondly, I have set the history of Greer against the background of a larger history: Mount Baldy and the parkland that extends from the White Mountains; and the Springerville-Eagar area, referred to as "Round Valley." From the beginning, the people of Greer have trafficked between many different places—by horse; team and wagon; and later, by cars and trucks. To become familiar with the settlement's past, it seems appropriate to consider it in relationship to the people, conditions, and events in the environs.

In particular, I acknowledge my debt to Atella Wiltbank Haws (Mrs. Carl), Mae Hale Wiltbank (Mrs. Milo), Afton Haws Wiltbank (Mrs. John Cleveland), and Vince Butler, to whom I have gone many times and asked, "What about this?"—and to Alice Lloyd who suggested people to contact. I also appreciate the help and encouragement offered by Dr. Charles C. Colley, Head of the Arizona Collection, Hayden Library, Arizona State University, Tempe. And to my friends and family, especially my husband Sam who has helped in so many countless ways to make the possibility, a reality—go my heart-felt thanks.

Karen Miller Applewhite
June, 1979
Phoenix, Arizona

Prologue

My cousin and I scooted back on the wooden seat, dusted with ashes that had been dumped down the two holes in an effort to smother the identifying smell of "outhouse," in the otherwise thoroughly satisfactory structure up the hill from our cabin. Big flies buzzed furiously in the open doorway, biting our bare thighs as we followed the mysterious journeys of exotic spiders that had squeezed out of cracks.

Our thick braids fell on branding-iron shirts from Goldwater's Store in Phoenix, and untried levis stacked stiffly on sensible Buster Brown shoes. The whole thing was held together, usually, by a Western belt with enormous embossed tin buckle.

We were transformed cowgirls, green, but undaunted—discussing plans and conquests for the summer season in Greer. Kathleen and I were close in age and pretty much agreed to agree, at least when we were together. I always thought we had our best discussions up there—side by side, elbows on knees, chins on palms, feet barely touching. (The problem with "hers" was it only had one hole. It was hard to carry on a real conversation because her outhouse was close enough to the road that one of us had to stand guard outside the door.)

Outside, the sun reached far to the bottom of the hill as it met the road, then dazzled the stream; its rays bending up against the opposite mountain. As far as our eyes could see were pine and aspen, grasses and flowers, and it never occurred to us not to think of it as ours.

The only unfamiliar thing was the saddle rack that had been built in the outhouse. My Uncle Tom said when he was little they used to keep a horse named "Rose" in a little wire corral up the hill. She was rented from the Wiltbanks in Eagar, year after year, and about the only trouble they ever had was when she was pregnant and bit him in the stomach; and when she didn't watch her step as he rode her over the wooden cattle guards. Of course there wasn't much margin for error in that situation. The only thing I could think was Rose must have had one set of uphill legs shorter than her downhill legs because that mountainside was as steep as the good Lord could make it and still get the trees to stand up straight.

Our cabin was the last one on the west fork road, up on the hill on Forest Service land, just before you got to Government Springs. "Little Nantucket," my grandfather called it. He was George H. Coffin from Phoenix and somehow related the whole thing to Nantucket Island (Massachusetts), whaling ships, and a heritage he knew of mostly on paper. He and my grandmother had six children and built the cabin in 1929, just as everyone was going off to college, getting married, and having children—all except my Uncle Tom. He was the end of the line, seven years younger than the next one up, and "had" to go up there. He and my grandmother would stay all summer with Claude, an Indian who worked for the family and tried (without much success) to find ways to get sent back to Phoenix because he liked to have a nip or two, and that was hard to come by in Greer. Granddaddy liked the idea of the whole place, but when it came to *being* there, he got a little bored. His custom was to come for the weekend (which must have been a trick in those days), and search for pitch knots to make roaring fires that would send people to the far end of the forty-foot room.

Some of my grandfather's sisters and a brother had come with their families and bought land north of our cabin. They went together and built a large community cabin with a living-dining room, kitchen for a cook (hired), and a guest bedroom, plus individual sleeping cabins for each family involved: the Will Coffins, Elias S. Clarks, Joseph Starks, all of Phoenix; Dr. and Mrs. P. G. Cornish, their son and his wife, Dr. Gillette and Dora Cornish, all of Albuquerque. The main cabin was finished in 1925. The "community plan" worked for one year, then each took to their individual sleeping quarters.

The cabin that belonged to my cousin's parents (the Harold C. Deckers) and grandparents (the Will Coffins) was built two feet from the main road. The location wasn't quite what they had in mind, but what was done was not to be undone—at least not until the CCC boys rerouted the road in the late 1930s.

We mostly avoided cabins during the day—unless it was raining. Then we might give theatricals, swathed in old ruffled bedspreads and dresser covers and making our delivery from the mezzanine; play bank with muffin tins for change and the huge fireplace screen for the tellers' cage; or get into marathon Monopoly games; or play Captain Marvel flying off the hammock on the front porch; or cook up something really gooey like fudge on the wood stove.

Our best thing was to be down by the stream—damming it up, diverting it into old channels, revving up a couple of stagnant tributaries, or arranging for a new waterfall or two. When that was done we'd fix up rooms in the willows and get very angry if clumsy fishermen didn't recognize our home for what it was. As we grew, there was also a good deal of posing on logs down there—waiting for some blond braves to come crashing through the thicket.

My brother John was generally down at the village, slopping hogs, pitching hay, or riding in trucks or on horses—getting in on things that were *definitely* not open to girls. (For a long time in my life, that seemed to include almost everything!) The mile to the village was a long walk. Mostly what was available for girls was getting the mail down at Wiltbanks'; getting groceries at Crosbys' Store and sort of riding the rail on the porch of the store; or you could use the bathroom off the front porch of Butlers' Lodge and spend a lot of time in there.

The problem was there were always a lot of "regulars" on the front porch you had to get by. They sat in rocking chairs and on benches—supreme justices before whom the village passed in review. I thought at the time they were enormously old, wizened, gray-haired, with aquiline noses. (Later I remembered them as much younger and better looking.)

3

Behind the dining room of the lodge was the sitting room with the bear rug on the wall John Butler had shot and player piano someone said had been driven many, many miles. Somehow I never hit "the right time to play it" (whenever that was) and usually ended up looking at half-clothed African natives through the stereoscope which mysteriously combined the two different pictures on a stiff postcard into one scene with a three-dimensional effect.

Then I might linger at the town swing before reluctantly starting uphill for home. There was a place on the south edge of the meadow, almost a certain tree where the whole psychology changed—the price of living so far from the center of things. If I was going to run into anyone who was to offer me a ride, it would be before that tree; if a storm came up, the thunder never cracked, nor lightning ripped the sky before reaching that tree; if I began to think I'd never make it home, I always dropped the sack of groceries somewhere beyond that spot.

In late afternoon we might try our own music—stacks and stacks of 78 rpm records from the seventh century, played on a victrola of about the same vintage. I can remember John Charles Thomas on "God Bless America" and a whiney rendition of "Bye-Bye-Blackbird." The most up-to-date we had was the Andrews Sisters singing about "Johnny Fedora['s]" love affair with Alice Blue-Bonnet after being in the window of a department store together. Usually the needle ground into a groove and the song slowly moaned to a stop before the end.

After electricity came in, someone brought up an enormous radio with futuristic wood cabinet, bronze grillwork, and plastic push buttons. Usually what were taken to the cabin were things well beyond the point of working, and being phased into the category of "relic." (They were then hauled to the dump just before they acquired real antique value.) The dial promised you could reach about 1,700 different places in the world, either directly or via short wave, police channel, through the North Pole, or relayed by transoceanic steamer.

By punching all the buttons about seven in the evening you got mostly—static. As the evening wore on, however, the Bible Belt shot its messages from the Deep South out across the air waves, into the nooks and crannies of remote America—badly in need of redemption and ripe for conversion. "This is Clint, Texas—That's right, folks, Clint, Texas— That's C-L-I-N-T, and we want *you* to send tonight for your glow-in-the-dark, life-like statue of Jesus Christ with absolutely no obligation."

Then it was bedtime. The rats and bats had been waiting around all day and expected us to keep regular hours, becoming quite impatient if we didn't. The bats started flying back and forth the length of the main room—The lower we'd get, the lower they'd swoop. The rats had a traffic

4

pattern that seemed to criss-cross the entire cabin, including up the stairs to the mezzanine. I was sure some night they'd forget themselves and take a shortcut across my face. They sampled everything except the carefully-baited rat traps.

Those were the years of childhood, adolescence. I was one who spent a lot of time wondering why things were the way they were and why they might not be otherwise; and was periodically curious about other people, though I couldn't imagine how anyone else could be. And I wondered about all the times past, the way it used to be, and wondered if it really was the way they said. Mostly I didn't ask too many questions until later.

I grew to an adult, married, had children—never breaking up my love affair with the forest, the stream, all the old haunts. But we were pretty much to ourselves when we were kids—Often it was just my mother, brother, and myself up there with no car. If we were to get to know the people better, we needed to be closer to town. When the USFS lease expired and wasn't eligible for renewal, we were told to vacate the cabin. So when "Little Nantucket" was phased out, I wrote a poem, and went down the road looking for a new place.

Little Nantucket

Little Nantucket

The winter's melted, Little Nantucket,
Time to shed the shroud of hibernation,
Evict furry tenants from secret places in rafters, logs, and floors,
Open your darkness to spring's soft stirring.

Ready your galley, rooms public and private,
Shake the season's leavings from decking, rails, and steps,
Sail through glistening aspen, patches of lupin, paintbrush, and daisy—
An ever changing, changeless odyssey through too many summers.

We leave the melting valley's heat,
Climb on canyoned roads to reach your lofty perch,
Parched and dazed by city's chaos,
Caught short by the forgotten simplicity of your idyll.

Footsteps echo as I wander through your rooms,
The people, times, long since gone—
Grandmothers, grandfathers, aunts, and uncles—fathers,
The children we were so long ago.

Bread baking, candy boiling, fires crackling, light flickering
On muddy jeans, tangled fish lines, boots falling in tired wrinkles,
Stray checker pieces, Monopoly money, depleted decks of cards,
Rusted horseshoes, twisted wood knots, skulls from far off meadows.

Some fifty years you've stood your ground,
Forest-locked ark, a faithful covenant with each generation,
A good place to come to, go out from—
Refreshed, realigned, wiser than when we came.

Now they mean to scuttle you,
Having lived beyond the policy that regulates your life.
They can't find any sanction for keeping you afloat—
Lone frigate, clinging to this hillside harborage.

Your anchor sinks deep into my heart—
Catches, one of the plumblines of my life.
Scarred surface of what you are, compulsively cleared away,
Your inward grace floats free beyond their reach or understanding.

—Karen M. Applewhite
1974

I

From The End Of The Road— To The Top Of The Trail

Most people climb to Greer's 8,300-foot perch either through the Show Low-Springerville-Eagar route or the Show Low-Lakeside-Pinetop-McNary road. There are other ways to approach the little village—more adventuresome, circuitous—but State Highway 260 is the "front door" way in. Many modern machines—long sedans, high-clearance pickups, low-slung sports cars, lean-back motorcycles, multi-storied campers, shoe-box motor homes, pulling boats and motorbikes, strapped together with every variety of gear—converge into one stream of curiosity-anticipation as they take a right or left on to State 373, the Greer turnoff.

Beautiful vistas are recorded by the eye's camera—frame after frame, unmarred, uninterrupted by anything save United States Forest Service (USFS) white-on-brown signs posted along the roadside explaining this is a recreation area; and spelling out all the attendant regulations in both words and international symbols. For the town of Greer is a small patchwork of private land floating on a sea of USFS land—some 5,120 acres of forest land and lakes comprise the recreation area.[1]

As the road humps up over the last rise, one catches the panorama of the Little Colorado River and town that nestles along the edges of the valley. From the knoll, a road forks off to the left and banks along the east side of the valley; the other winds down across the river, into the main "business center." The structures, some decades old of log and board, notched and nailed together; some days old of multi-colored aluminum siding, just wheeled in, parked on a pad for the season, juxtapose along the west fork road.

First-timers duly note the quaint scene, locate the bars, game rooms, and gift shops, their accelerator foot cramping into lock at "twenty-five miles per hour," as they crane their necks around the next pine to see "where this road goes"—withholding a verdict until they find something big.

Neither fork of the road goes anywhere—except to the end of itself. That's not to say there are not places along the way or that Greer is a dead end, perhaps just a cul-de-sac as far as the average, tired, wheel-bound tourist goes. Some are just frustrated as heck to have to negotiate "a three-sixty" and sheepishly retrace their route, carefully averting their gaze as they pass the same faces, places; then on—endlessly—searching for the road through to anywhere.

Many, however, are delighted to find an excuse to go nowhere—to be trapped in this gorgeous dead end. But Greer is really only part way "there" in this country; and where the roads end, trails thread some seven miles up the canyons of both the east and west forks of the Little Colorado to the vast meadowland around Sheep's Crossing, Colter Reservoir, Phelp's Cabin. This is being "up on the mountain," not *the mountain,* because that's Mount Baldy. "Up on the mountain" is a generic term used locally, referring to the high plateau country sloping out from the base of the string of volcanic peaks, part of the Mogollon Range. The snow-capped White Mountains give their name to this whole recreational trapezoid—from Mount Baldy, northwest to Show Low, southeast to Springerville-Eagar, then to Alpine.

There are roads through this high country (including County 122 forking off from the Greer road), some newly cut for logging or recreational use, but many following old wagon tracks of the late 1800-1900s. People have been coming "up on the mountain," criss-crossing the plateaus for over a hundred years, mostly by horseback because it was shorter, quicker than the rocky, steep wagon roads up canyons, along river beds—driving sheep and cattle, hunting, fishing, seeking land, satisfying curiosity; establishing one or two room cabins to watch their stock, raise a little grain; pulling wagons of various sizes, for chuck, and assorted supplies for longer stays. Difficult routes out, over, or through the mountains of the valley towns such as Greer rarely stopped the pioneers. They just mounted a horse; or if by wagon, jettisoned part of the load in bogs or steep places (people or goods); laid a board track or hitched up another team of horses or people in front or back to get them up and out.

Also crossing the parkland is a grass-covered dike—not an ancient remnant—but once the rail-bed of the remarkable Apache Railway that linked McNary to Maverick, a townsite on the south slope of Mount Baldy at the confluence of Pacheta and Bluff Cienega Creeks. The town was created as a result of a contract between Southwest Forest Industries and the Fort Apache Indian Tribe giving the company use of reservation land for its logging operations. McNary and the lumber town were officially connected by sixty-eight miles of rail in the spring, 1949, when a 112-year-old Apache Chief named "Tipah" drove a copper spike at the end of the line.

The logging train made two round trips a day to McNary. It was only sixty-five (grueling) miles by dirt from McNary to Maverick; and a Maverick resident recalled that during June, their dustiest month, some tourists pulled into town fuzzy-brown with dirt, saying, "Thank heavens we finally made it to Greer!" Some billion board-feet later, on August 1, 1967 Maverick was "discontinued," dismantled—the rails, ties along its route removed, and its site no longer mistaken for Greer.[2]

It's easy to get side-tracked in this country. The trails cross road-bed, rail-bed, entering the Mount Baldy Wilderness, some 6,975 acres on the eastern slope of the mountain set aside in 1970 for travel by foot—either one's own, or those of a four-legged creature. Both east and west fork trails mainly follow the tributaries of the Little Colorado as they tumble, sometimes trickle, down beside the aisles shadowed by arching pines, spruce, firs that cut the sky into patches—a few shafts of light piercing the tracery of branch and bough, dappling ferns and flowers in a yellow glow.

The pilgrimage up the mountain is centuries old, if one believes stories of ancient Indians who came from far away, made this same journey through the protective forest, up on to the bald back of the mountain to honor their gods and make petitions. Ironically, the 11,590-foot peak is

11

within, by one-fourth mile, the Fort Apache Indian Reservation, and the summit is now "unreachable" unless one has a tribal permit (obtainable only in Whiteriver) to hike on its land—a regulation probably more political than religious in nature.[3]

On the northwest face of the quarter-mile saddle leading to the peak can still be found remnants of pottery—small gray, red, yellow, black stone beads, an occasional turquoise one; most about one-sixteenth in diameter, less than a thirty-second of an inch thick; and rarely, arrow points—all evidence of an ancient people. The meager plant life, short twisted bushes and trees, stunted by cold and wind, lead one to conjecture this was not their home, but a place to come for a limited time and purpose.

James Willard Schultz, prolific writer of Indian lore, *In The Great Apache Forest* (a story of George Crosby, a lone boy scout in Greer), tells how the priests would come from the desert near Oraibi to this spot to pray and perform mysteries in the Rain God's kiva while their people, hundreds and hundreds of them, camped in the nearby timber—praying and waiting. On the fourth day the people would come to the summit with their most valued things as a sacrifice to the Rain God.

> These they placed here and there upon this butte, the very highest point of this highest mountain of all the range, where Rain God loved to sit and look out upon the world, and some they placed around the entrance to his kiva, in which he often performed his great mysteries. And as they set them down upon the rocks they prayed him to accept their poor offerings and to drop his rain plentifully upon their plantings. Men taught their little sons and mothers their little daughters to say those prayers, and guided their little hands in the placing of their toy offerings. Why, in that long-ago time this whole butte was covered with gifts to Rain God: beautiful ollas; bead necklaces; the finest clothing; weapons; children's buzzers, dolls, and other toys.[4]

The pile of rocks that marks the top of the mountain has known the tread of many white men. More modern pilgrims, on a summer weekend day as many as fifty, record in a dog-eared, pencil-smudged notebook secured in a metal box that long ago ran out of pages: "Never again!"; "Seventeenth annual hike"; "Alleluia, Praise the Lord!"; "Made it in one hour, fifteen minutes"; "Nothin' to it"; "Out of sight!"

Also jutting out of the rocks are remnants of the eight-sided, eight-windowed, conical-roofed building that was used as a lookout station during the early 1900s. It was tiny, according to Schultz, just large enough for a central chart stand, small stove, one chair, and telephone. To the northeast, near a spring, was a little log cabin used by rangers—a 10x12-foot room with two windows and 4x6-foot porch attached.[5] *In The Great Apache Forest,* George and his sister Hannah Crosby were deputized rangers for the summer of 1917, stationed on the mountain, and in the course of their adventures tracked down some menacing "fire-bugs."

Mount Baldy

This forest is part of the largest continuous stand of ponderosa pine in the United States extending from the Mogollon Mountains in New Mexico to the San Francisco Peaks near Flagstaff. Baldy's virgin forest of Englemann and blue spruce, fir, quaking aspen, and mixed conifer has never been logged (excluding the portion on the reservation). From the slopes, or at the foot of the mountain are the headwaters of major rivers and streams including the Little Colorado, the White, the Black, Paradise, and Ord. Mule and white tail deer, elk, black bear, turkey, blue grouse, squirrel, and rabbit are part of the resident population as well as seasonal cattle that graze within the wilderness.[6]

Within our view, if not within our life-span, passed early explorer-adventurers—searching for new routes, riches from the virgin land: Coronado with his Spanish soldiers, hundreds of Indians, horses, cattle, and sheep, left Mexico in about 1540 in search of the legendary Cities of Cibola (seven cities containing vast treasures established in the unexplored world by an old world bishop) and is believed to have passed through Little Colorado country near present day McNary on his way to Zuni, in what is now New Mexico.[7]

James Ohio Pattie wrote in *Personal Narrative* of his trapping expeditions in the White Mountains in 1826. Beaver pelts, weighing several pounds apiece, were in high demand. Hairs from the soft underfur made fine felt. According to *Arizona Place Names,* Pattie explored some eighty miles south and east of the head of Salt River, calling the fork "Black River," its canyons—some 1,200-1,500 feet deep—reputed by mountain men to be the worst in the whole range.[8]

The initial surveys in this part of the New Mexico Territory, acquired from Mexico in 1848, which most closely corresponded to what eventually became the Black Mesa Forest Reserve (later the Sitgreaves and Apache National Forests) were made by Captain Lorenzo Sitgreaves of the Corps of Topographical Engineers, U.S. Army. He set out from Zuni in 1851; followed the Zuni River to its junction with the Little Colorado near present St. Johns; mapping a possible route for a proposed railroad eventually to connect the Atlantic coast to the Pacific.[9]

The vista—velvet-soft blue-green mounds, pockets filled here and there with cobalt-blue lakes—silences the bloody history of "Apacheria." During the 1860s there were few white men north of the Gila and Salt Rivers, no roads to speak of in Northern Arizona, and the Apache Indians controlled the mountain zone of eastern and central Arizona. This paradise through which Indian Scout Al Sieber (from Germany) led his 30-100 scouts contained flocks of wild turkey he estimated at ten thousand birds; in which his scouts might kill eighty deer in a day, was still the setting of Indian outbursts.[10]

Sometimes referred to as a "paradise for devils," the mid-1800s saw this part of the New Mexico Territory (The Territory of Arizona was created in 1863.) virtually unguarded from Indian backlash or from outlaws who began to flourish in this no-man's land. Military protection and the forts were abandoned during the Civil War; the Indians regained control; and miners, ranchers either fled to safer parts, or took things into their own hands.

> From 1864 to 1874 the history of Arizona was written in blood. Isolated from the world and with the most imperfect and irregular means of communication, population increased slowly; the few who had the hardihood to run the risk of the tomahawk and the scalping knife were attracted by the rich mineral discoveries in Northern Arizona and that portion of the territory received the larger portion of the immigration ... In the ten years [between 1864-74] it is estimated not less than one-thousand victims of savage atrocity found bloody graves in Arizona ... [The pioneer coming into the fertile valleys and rich bottom lands] tilled the soil with his trusty rifle strapped to the plow and his

ready six shooter belted about him ... If a stock owner, he had to maintain an armed guard day and night around his herd.[11]

Fort Apache (having undergone several early name-changes) was established in 1870 near the confluence of the east and north forks of the White River as a means of avoiding the malaria prevalent in old Camp Goodwin at the end of the Gila Valley. By Executive Order, the 1,681,920 acre Fort Apache Indian Reservation was established on November 9, 1871. (At a later date, part of the reservation was separated to form the San Carlos Indian Reservation.)[12] The road linking the two posts became part of the military trail extending through Fort Defiance on the Navajo Reservation to Fort Wingate near Gallup, New Mexico.

The campaign against the Apaches was resumed by the War Department and "... continued until all renegade bands were run down, captured or killed, the number of troops stationed at the fourteen [major] army posts in Arizona was increased from a few hundred men at first to upward of six thousand officers and men at the end, one-fourth of the regular army."[13]

Martha Summerhays, telling of her stay at (then) Camp Apache as the young wife of an army officer, wrote:

> They [the Indians in 1874] were divided into bands ...; they came into the post twice a week to be counted, and to receive their rations of beef, sugar, beans, and other staples, which Uncle Sam's commissary officer issued to them ... Large stakes were driven into the ground; at each stake, sat or stood the leader of a band; a sort of father to his people; then the rest of them stretched out in several long lines, young bucks and old ones, squaws and pappooses, the families together, about seventeen hundred souls in all.[14]

Because Arizona had no railroad connections at this time, the problem of feeding the troops and Indians was serious. To meet the needs, cattle had to be driven in from states and territories to the east, as well as forage and food provided. Some of the Apaches who were friendly provided tons of "hay" (native grass) for Fort Apache which they brought in on their backs, cutting as much as fifteen tons on some days, and most of it was cut with old knives or pieces of tin or iron. "These same Apaches furnished the new military camp with wood, droves of them sometimes bringing in as much as thirty cords in one day ... cut with dull axes or broken with rocks and packed on their backs."[15]

The army officers were impressed by the beauty of the mountains. In 1873 Capt. George M. Wheeler established a camp on what he called "Thomas Peak" (later "Mount Baldy") and called the view one of " 'the most magnificent and effective of any among the large number that have come under my observation ... Few world-wide travelers in a lifetime even could be treated to a more perfect landscape, a true virgin solitude, undefiled by the presence of man.' "[16] Other adjacent peaks, "Green's," "Ord," as well as "Thomas" were named for army officers.

Mountain and military men, Indians, an occasional settler made their way across this vast plateau, through sometimes tortuous canyons and trees often described as "thick as hair on a dog's back"—some scratching the itch to explore, some fighting the engulfing tide of pale-face civilization, some trying to tame the country for "civilized" purposes.

II

Who Were They And How'd They Get There?

Much of the "settling down" and "in" during the last century was along waterways and within rich bottom lands. What is known today as "Round Valley" (Springerville-Eagar), bordered on the south, west, and east by mountains; mesas on the north and west, broken by the scattered green of cinder hills in the northwest, comprises what has been called the land of fifty extinct volcanoes.

During the 1860-70s came the first bona fide Spanish and Anglo settlers—"sold" on the beauty and potential of the bowl-shaped valley. They trickled in slowly at first—then with the Mormon wagon trains from Utah, more steadily as they claimed land; grazed their stock over the White Mountain country; and from this center, out of this nucleus, extended trails into other valleys in the vicinity: Nutrioso, Alpine, and Greer. (The latter two were early known as "Bush Valley" and "Lee Valley.")

From ancient ruins and numerous artifacts not far below the surface of Round Valley's floor, surrounding cliffs and canyons, the presence of Indians long ago is certain. Why they came or left is a matter of conjecture, but because the area had been referred to by Indians as "Chinte" or "Devil Valley," it is supposed something calamitous took place there—It became "off limits," and the natives left rather precipitously. Most old-timers confirm that as long back as they can remember, Indians seemed superstitious about, and skirted Round Valley.[1]

The first comers found the land free, unencumbered—part of what was known as the public domain. Forester-historian Fred Winn noted, "They were individualists to the core with unbounded faith in themselves and in their destiny."[2] The resources of this domain were free for the taking if one had the stamina to grab, hold, and defend them—from mineral rights; to forage for livestock; timber and logs for building, fencing, and fuel; water for irrigation, and as a source of power. The creatures of the air, streams, lakes, forest, and prairie were free—to be caught, shot, eaten without limit.

Most of the early locations (of the Mormons) along the Little Colorado were based on squatters' rights, since prior to 1879 none of the land had been surveyed or officially opened to homesteading.[3] Various means were devised to show one's claims, especially for sites seasonally occupied. Being *present* was the most persuasive means of "ownership," but other methods were controlling the water, building cabins, and sheep troughs; laying out logs in a square to show intent of building; planting peach or plum pits on the perimeter of the land (As they first blossomed, they became a sign of occupancy.); or piling rocks along the corners. For a stockman, "the unwritten law of the range was he who first watered his stock at the stream, spring, or water hole had the prior and exclusive right to use thereafter, together with such adjoining range lands as he could use."[4]

The White Mountain land was soon opened to homesteading privileges which essentially meant a single citizen could take up to 160 acres outside government land, or up to eighty acres within limits of a railroad grant or government area; and after continuous residence and cultivation for five years, and upon payment of a small fee, gain absolute title. Another was "An Act to Encourage the Growth of Timber on Western Prairies," and stipulated planting trees on twenty acres out of eighty or ten out of forty, and continuing their growth for eight years before receiving good title. (George H. Crosby, early Mormon bishop in Round Valley, received land in the upper end of Eagar after planting and growing locusts.) Various exemptions were added during the course of "homesteading" which led to an influx of speculators in some areas. One exemption made land available six months after filing for $1.25 an acre.[5]

Another difficulty "after the fact" came as the railroads reached the territory: The government offered the Atlantic and Pacific (brought through Joseph City to the northwest in 1881) forty square miles of land for each mile of track laid in Arizona Territory. Many of the railroad sections were bought by big cattle outfits. By leasing the alternate public domain sections, the cattle companies were able to control huge areas, many of which were tentatively held by small settlers prior to the advent of the railroad. By opening up areas, bringing them out of isolation, the railroad at the same time hastened settlement by thousands of immigrants attracted to the West.

The first people to enter what they called "Valle Redondo" came unencumbered, unaware of any Anglo land regulations. They spoke Spanish and came from the Rio Grande to the east, driving their sheep into summer pastures in Arizona. The first man to settle in the valley was probably Juan Baca who came in 1862 as a twenty-year-old. He later brought his mother, Maria Trujillo Baca, and brothers Dionicio, Francisco, and Benino.

A Castillo family soon followed, building a rock fort for protection against Indians in a grove of trees at the lower end of the valley. (The women and children stayed in the 8x8-foot fort during scares, while the men climbed the nearby ridge to watch and shoot from behind rock barricades they had built there.) These Spanish families together with others that followed farmed beans, squash, corn, chili, and potatoes; and as a later settler remembered, cut their hay with butcher knives and scythes. A man who later became one of the largest sheepowners and taxpayers in Yavapai County, Juan Candelaria, drove seven hundred head from New Mexico to a ranch site near Concho in 1866.

In what was to be later named "Springerville," the lands were first held by these Spanish. Dionicio Baca homesteaded 160 acres; and not until additional patented land held by Eulalio Baca and Senon Castillo was broken up into small tracts, did the town grow.[6]

The first Anglos to come into the valley were William R. (Tony) Milligan, Johnny McCullough, and Tony Long. They established themselves in 1869-70 at the upper end of the valley. The first map of Arizona (Colton's, 1873) shows Round Valley as "Milligan's Fort."

19

Castillo Fort
- Round Valley

Milligan was an enterprising sort. He established the first saw and grist mills; had a large farm, the first year raising 800,000 pounds of barley which he sold to the army at Fort Apache for five-and-one-half cents per pound and made a good profit. He, together with Tony Long, had the contract to erect houses for White Mountain Apaches (each costing the government $1,600, in which the Indians housed their livestock while they preferred living in their wickiups); and was a major freighter in association with Solomon Barth of St. Johns—their teams and wagons going between Trinidad, Colorado and Albuquerque, and to army posts such as Fort Apache. Milligan's sawmill was the first that converted timber into lumber from the virgin White Mountain stands. The mill was fed its first log in October, 1876.

The next arrival, in 1873, was a party of three from Wisconsin which included James G. H. Colter. He settled briefly in Round Valley, then acquired vast holdings around Nutrioso and vicinity. Colter played an influential part in Round Valley, however, as one of the area's first cattlemen; first deputy U.S. Marshal of the district; as an elected member of the 1879 Territorial Legislature that had "Apache County" carved out of Yavapai with Springerville becoming seat of the new county after the election of 1880; and finally, as a married man—establishing the Colter-Rudd dynasty through his marriage with Rosa Rudd, daughter of William M. and Eliza Catherine Rudd.[7]

Julius Becker came in 1874 from Belen, New Mexico where he and his brother Gustav had been employed by the stage coach operators who covered the territory from the end of the Santa Fe Railroad in Las Animas, Colorado to El Paso, Texas—the coaches passing through Santa Fe, Albuquerque, Belen, Socorro, and other towns on the route. The imagination of the two young men from the province of Hanover, Germany was fired by tales of wonderful grazing on the plains and adjacent mountains told by several men returning from Arizona Territory. (These men who had enthusiastically recommended A.T. were later "detained" by the Texas Rangers for cattle rustling.)

Gustav arrived on horseback on August 26, 1876 (another twenty-year-old), with all his worldly possessions: horse, saddle, the clothes he wore, and a Winchester rifle. Along the route from the (later) rail-head in Trinidad, Colorado, he and his Mexican guide had shared their scant supply of food with a group of four foot-travelers. Consequently, the two had nothing to eat the last days of their journey. During the trip Becker and his guide were held off at gunpoint by an Arizona-bound party from Arkansas who feared their families might be attacked by the grimy, gaunt men.[8]

Ironically, Gustav Becker and the Arkansas party arrived in town about the same time. In the latter group were the first families to the area as well as its first doctor, Dr. William Mann Rudd, his wife, Catherine; all or most of their twelve children; a brother, Jim Rudd and family; and a Bush family. In her life story, Eliza Catherine Rudd remarked that Prescott was the nearest county seat (which took seven days to reach), and "Springerville was not much of a place, there were four white men and their wives, and the rest were Mexicans."[9]

Though Julius had been farming—raising grain to sell at Fort Apache—after Gustav arrived in the outlaw-infested camp in the wilderness, they began their mercantile business. This store grew to become a many-faceted enterprise in later years. From a ledger entry, their first sale was made in March, 1876 to one of the Bacas. Oxen were used for the 160-mile trip to Belen on the Rio Grande where Gustav and Julius arranged with their brother John to buy goods on credit, and store them until the wagons arrived from Springerville—a one and one-half to two-month trip. (Some freighted the 250 miles, one way, to Albuquerque.) Since there was no post office in Round Valley, this was also the mail route. When the brothers were able to gather cash from transactions with money-starved settlers, they would stuff gold coins and greenbacks in

(Dovetail-log) Grain Warehouse for
the Beckers- Built
in Springerville ca. 1878-

saddle bags and boots, ride east at night, announcing a different depar-
ture date than planned to avoid the outlaws who always followed them
once they were "missed" from the store.

Sometimes the Beckers "carried" settlers for several years in the
cash-scarce economy. About the only money available was paid by the
army for contracts to supply Fort Apache with barley, oats, hay, and
wood. Farmers would get credit on their Becker bill by freighting the
sixty-four miles over the top of the mountain through Cluff Cienega (later
"McNary"), by Cooley's Ranch (five miles south of present Pinetop), to
Fort Apache. The haul took six to twelve days depending on weather.
During the 1870-80s, customers might pay on their bills by bringing in
quarters of bear, elk, and deer. Buckskin was also legal tender.[10]

A. V. Greer, namesake of "Greer," Harris Phelps and families were
the first Mormons in the area, coming in 1877 in wagons from Texas.
Americus Vespucious Greer (who survived a twin brother, Christopher
Columbus!) was known as Uncle "H" after serving as captain of Company
H during the Civil War. Also reknowned as a Texas Ranger, A. V. Greer
was remembered as a picturesque figure, with white hair standing up on
his head, a great white beard, and deep-set eyes. Another brother,

Thomas Lacy Greer, established a vast cattle outfit with headquarters near Hunt, north of Concho. A. V. Greer soon held important positions in the developing church and laid out the town of Amity in the upper end of the valley.

The first Mormons in Round Valley settled east of present Springerville along Nutrioso Creek. As their need for more land increased, they scraped irrigation ditches "up on the bench," and moved their settlements to the southwest, in the upper end of the valley.

During the same year (1877) William J. Flake, known as the church trader, and herd boys, John Burk and Adam Greenwood, came looking for land and water in preparation for the coming of the "saints" from Utah. He was able to secure forty acres of standing corn in the valley. The year before, Brigham Young had called 200 families out of Utah to establish themselves along the Little Colorado River in Arizona Territory. Their route was blazed by Jacob Hamblin in 1873, from southern Utah to the Little Colorado and up the river into its headwaters—the "territory" of Springerville, Eagar, Nutrioso, Alpine, Greer. In 1878, Hamblin brought his family to Springerville and founded the first Mormon ward.[11]

Part of that Mormon route was remembered by a nephew, Thomas Howell Hamblin, who arrived in Round Valley on January 1, 1880:

> It took us three days to ferry 300 head of cattle across the Colorado River. On December 7 the last cow was on the east side of the river and we climbed over Lee's Backbone, a steep, rocky ridge about 1,000 feet above the river bed . . .[12]

Their trip took thirty-one days from "Pahreah" (forty miles north of Lee's Ferry) to Round Valley. A later traveler remembered the treacherous drop-off on either side of the "backbone" and as the brakes couldn't be trusted, the wheels had to be tied solid.

In their preparations, pioneers gave special attention to draft stock and wagons—bringing an assortment of horses, oxen, mules, and cattle. The weight limit was figured at about two thousand pounds per wagon. Women and children would bounce on top of the wagons loaded with household goods, grain for seed purposes, staple food, and. tools. One bachelor who came into Arizona with Lot Smith in 1876, listed as essential:

> $50.00 in cash, 4 oxen, one wagon, one plane, hoe, pitchfork, crow bar, one rifle, two barrels of nails, one bucket, milk pan, and strainer, lantern, bake and camp kettle, a fry pan, two tin plates and cups, knives, forks, and spoons, four blankets and a bed, two pair of shoes, and three pair of

boots, four bu. wheat, 1½ bu. of potatoes, 500 lbs. of flour, 40 gal. of molasses, 20 lbs. of apples, one ham and six lbs. of butter, 4 lbs. of candles, 9 lbs. of soap, 16 boxes of matches and some garden seed.[13]

Often the load included organs, pianos, wood ranges, and sewing machines, which might have to be sacrificed along the trail to lighten the load.

Despite the hardship, disease, and disaster (not to mention child-birth), travel over the Mormon wagon road was heavy.

During the early years, supply wagons lumbered the three hundred miles from southern Utah to supplement the meager production of Little Colorado farms. Over it came the livestock which served as a medium of exchange in the Mormon land purchases and as foundation herds. Over it, too, moved churchmen, polygamists, wedding entourages, and jaded missionaries returning to Zion. Many settlers made the trip numerous times.[14]

When they arrived, the settlers would often live in their wagon boxes until forts (usually a self-contained clustering of cabins around a commu-

Bringing Home Logs

nity building of some sort) were built and they could move in. Sometimes the wagon boxes were taken off the running gears, set on rocks or logs; while the gears were used for hauling logs from nearby forests to put up the typical one or two room log cabin that was "home." It would usually have a hardened dirt floor and door and window openings covered with the wagon cover. Women could then set about housekeeping which included making soap, cheese, butter, medicines, spinning, curing meat, and "making do" from the meager and often expensive resources at hand.

Not knowing what to expect, the Mormon people nonetheless approached from a colonizing perspective and they were as well equipped physically, psychologically, religiously, for the hardships ahead as any people who came. As an organized, cohesive, co-operative force, they often encountered intense resistance, even hatred, by "outsiders" suspicious of the saints' numbers, ways, and potential as a political conglomerate. This resistance—sometimes justified, more often not—was met with courage, patience, and practicality.

One of the hottest issues was the Mormon practice of polygamy. Some seven thousand Mormons lived in Arizona Territory in 1884 and one-half of Apache County's whites were Mormons. The polygamists, particularly, were the subject of attack by the *Apache Chief,* St. Johns, Apache County, Arizona Territory: "a 32 column paper published ... by George A. McCarter every Friday. It is an anti-Mormon Journal being the only one in the Territory." (March 28, 1884) Some of the newspaper's pleas were:

> Something must be done [by legislative action] by which the Territory can be kept pure and unsullied ... if some means are not resorted to then Arizona will take its stand by the side of Utah in the great calamity of Mormon domination. [April 4, 1884]

> The Mormon love of land is notorious. He takes it wherever it can be found and he is not very particular about his methods in getting it. [May 23, 1884]

> [In speaking of Gentiles sticking together against 'these beastly inclined Mormons,' the editor noted that ordinary Mormons could only afford one wife, but were being encouraged otherwise by bishops, in order to make the officials' practices look good.] It is the elders who keep houses full of wives, the rich old bishops that have accumulated large fortunes out of the church tithes, and who can afford this luxury. [July 11, 1884]

The anti-polygamy movement culminated in 1884 with five men being brought to trial at Prescott, several fined, and imprisoned. A piece of territorial legislation briefly took the vote away from polygamists and anyone who believed in the doctrine.[15] Hundreds of Mormons fled to Mexico to avoid prosecution, or moved families to other locales to maintain the appearance of monogamy. One early settler in Round Valley who was a polygamist left by foot for Old Mexico, where his family later joined him.

Another one of the brethren who arrived in 1879 and who was important in the story of Greer was Ellis Whitney Wiltbank. He and his father, Spencer W., came to look at the feasibility of locating in the valley. Spencer Watson returned in 1880 with five of his children.[16] In 1882, "Ett" (as E.W.W. was called) returned with his family, settling in Nutrioso. Ett then moved to "Union," (later "Eagar Ward") in 1889. From the ranks of Ellis Whitney's family, his brothers and sisters, sons and daughters, came much of the "glue" that held Greer together and made it work.

One of the inescapable facts of life in the White Mountains in those days was the outlaw element which pretty well ran things. Between horse stealing and cattle rustling, coming to town to let off a little steam built up by whiskey, and terrorizing the "tourists," they discouraged traffic and settlement by all but the stout-hearted. The Clantons of Tombstone fame had their headquarters east of Springerville and always came in for mail. When they came for "other things," they were oftentimes driven off by threat of Gustav Becker's fully-loaded six-shooter which he kept for a lifetime in his old-fashioned pigeonhole desk.

Besides the Clantons were the Cavanaugh or Snider gang, nine of whom fell after a shoot-out on the hill back of the Eagar cemetery; the Westbrooks; and upon occasion, Billy the Kid. Many of these had been driven out of the territory to the east by the relentless pursuit of the Texas Rangers—into the no-man's land of the Arizona Territory. When Commodore P. Owens became sheriff of Apache County in September, 1887 he was given indictments by a grand jury in Prescott against the worst of the outlaws. Half of the lot were tendered their summons posthumously.[17]

Though the term "Apache" was a conglomerate applied to several different groups including the often peaceful White Mountain tribes, people "had heard" of so many attacks, ambushes, they were intimidated and constantly on guard. Willmirth G. DeWitt, A. V. Greer's daughter, said, "We used to be greatly alarmed on account of the Indians, as this was when Geronimo, the great Apache warrior was on the warpath."[18] (The Apaches who raided mostly for horses, avoided Round Valley because it was so open, with few trees for protection.)

Particularly vivid were accounts of Victorio, San Carlos Indian chief, who with a band went on a rampage in 1880, led the Alma massacre, and the massacre and burning of Quemado (first known as "American Valley" in New Mexico). During this "outing" they camped just across the New Mexico line, twenty miles from Bush Valley. The band stayed there killing beef, drying meat, while raiding parties stole horses all around the country. Then, Thomas H. Hamblin wrote:

> One afternoon about four o'clock they [his two half-brothers] were driving the horses to the corral when about 15 Indians rode out of the timber on a dead run. Each Indian was riding a cavalry horse and saddle and carrying an army rifle in his right hand, high above his head, holding the reins with his left hand. They had red bandanas around their heads.
>
> When the boys looked around, the Indians started yelling and trying to cut the boys off from the fort, and they would have succeeded had not their horses struck a bog. They mired to their knees when about 30 yards away. The Indians took 63 head of horses, but the boys got away.[19]

By 1886 with the surrender of Geronimo, the rounding up and shipping off of many of the Apache bands, vigilance was relaxed.

The great iron horse did as much as anything else to tame the country, connect it with "civilization," as the Atlantic and Pacific (later the "Santa Fe") pushed across northern Arizona in the 1880s. Into the country came the first great herds of cattle and as a direct or indirect consequence, the eventual extinction of the grizzly bear and great herds of native Merriam elk and diminishment of the flocks of Merriam turkey. (Al Sieber and his scouts had spoken of using just breasts from gobblers weighing up to forty pounds for jerky.) The Beckers freighted elk and bear meat to the crews laying tracks for the railroad. They employed a crew of twelve hunters in the late 1870-80s who killed game to sell to the Atlantic and Pacific. Elk brought $1.75 per quarter and bear, $1.50 per quarter. Prior to cattle—elk, deer, bear, turkey provided about all the fresh meat people had.[20]

The railroad brought the Aztec Land and Cattle Co. and the Hashknife brand to Arizona Territory—some 60,000 head came by rail in

the summer and fall of 1885, and spring of 1886. George H. Crosby, Jr. (Apache County Superior Court Judge), wrote in the *St. Johns Observer* (March 1, 1924), "They came with their long Texas horns, long and slim like race horses, with big-necked bulls almost like buffaloes ... It took forty cowboys to brand the calves, ride the bogs, guard against cattle rustlers and round up the steers and barren cows for market, while the horse wrangler had over four-hundred head of saddle horses to take care of when the roundup was busy." The name of the brand was said to stem from the big knives the cowboys used for skinning cattle and cutting up food at chuck time.

The same writer recalls the "old Twenty-Four" of Henry Smith, Ernest Tee, and (later,) Thomas Carson that came in with 1,800 head just prior to the railroad; made its home ranch between St. Johns and Springerville; with a horse camp on the mountain west of Greer. Smith and Tee were a pair of Englishmen of wealth, education, and refinement—Carson, a blunt, gruff Scotchman. Both the Hashknife and Twenty-Four's herds were vastly reduced during the droughts of the early 1890s and Crosby noted that dead cattle made the Little Colorado fairly rotten with carcasses.

The cattle, some almost wild, weighing only five or six hundred pounds, would range into steep country, especially since there were no fences. The number of outfits—their brands, earmarks, and range published weekly in the St. Johns newspaper—increased. Though some outfits folded (i.e., the Hashknife) at the turn of the century, and despite discouragement over fluctuating prices, drought, and unseasonable freezes, an important tradition of the region had been established.

With Coronado came the first cattle into Arizona and the United States, though they didn't survive as they were used to feed the soldiers on their trek. With the longhorns in the late 1880s came the qualities needed to survive the drives and the terrain: They could run like deer, keep up with a horse, and were able to cover as much as twenty miles in a day. But as ranchers began to look for something more than horns and bone, they turned to the breed that was to dominate on the ranges during the next century—the Hereford.[21]

III

They Wouldn't Stay Put

He could always see something brighter on the other side of the fence and so he moved away.
[Afton Wiltbank of her father-in-law, Ellis Whitney Wiltbank][1]

If cliches become threadbare from overuse, perhaps it's because there's so much truth in them: The grass might have looked a little greener out Lee Valley way, especially as there weren't even fences to hurdle. At any rate, wagon ruts and horse trails led to the area sixteen miles southwest of Round Valley as early as 1879, perhaps earlier. The first (Lee Valley) settlers probably just passed through the Springerville-Eagar settlement and went higher up looking for unencumbered land. Some were simply hunting for a summer place to raise crops, graze their herds—returning to lower elevations for the winter. In seeking new places they were bound by little but availability and physical limitations of the locations. Charles S. Peterson in *Take Up Your Mission: Mormon Colonizing Along the Little Colorado River, 1870-1900* says:

> Although land comprised an important element in the Mormon value system and was the basis of a colony's exis-

tence, its hold upon individuals was generally not great. In fact by comparison to the values in high-cost property situations, most Little Colorado settlers displayed a remarkable casualness toward specific parcels of land. As newcomers to the region their sentimental attachments were not yet deeply seated, and allegiance could be, and was, shifted with surprising frequency .... Unfettered by large investment or success, it was easy to look beyond the next hill, and the record is replete with accounts of families—including those most loyal to the church—pulling up stakes again and again, with scarcely a glance behind, and moving to new premises.[2]

It is doubtful anyone paid for rights to Lee Valley, later "Greer"—they just set up camp. First among those who came was Amberion Englevson, who must have been a hard man to pin down: First, because his name and nationality was so variously spelled out and secondly, because his story has been told in so many ways. He was either a Norwegian, Frenchman, or something else; was either "Amberon Englevalson," "Heber Dolton Amberion," "Ambijorn Engualsen," or "Amburing Engvoltzing"! and came with his horses to a place on the flat, at the south end of the meadow where the east and west forks of the Little Colorado join.

Some say he was a freighter and raised the first grain in the valley. Since a threshing machine wasn't known of then, he built a round corral, tramped the ground hard, then drove horses over the grain, cleaning it by winnowing in the wind. He built a little one-room cabin and was believed to have slept there with his horses to keep warm. Most accounts agree on his end: He was killed by a horse near Springerville. What he left, besides his first name which has been applied to the point of land above where he settled ("Amberion Point"), was gold—or at least so the story goes. Many a child and probably adult, has dug around the mound of stones that was once his fireplace looking for the treasure. A more recent owner of the property warns, "Now they're liable to run into the septic tank if they go diggin' too deep![3]

The second (and perhaps third) person(s) one hears of in Lee Valley, whose story has undoubtedly also been enhanced by time, is Tommy Lang who is said to have homesteaded and lived on the old Norton place (a spoon-shaped valley southwest of the Greer turn-off). He took water out of Squirrel Creek to irrigate crops, and later Squirrel Creek was called "Lang." When John Alfred Norton acquired the place is not known. Perhaps he took it up in partnership with Lang, or perhaps Lang was simply the tenant. At any rate, Lang was shot and killed by a Smith, Carson and Co., Twenty-Four cowboy named Youngblood.

Fireplace at the Old Norton Place

John A. Norton was among the original groups of Mormon settlers who came to the upper Little Colorado from Utah. He and his wife Theresa raised grain (wheat and oats), and potatoes on the Norton Ranch in the late 1800s. (Seed potatoes were brought from Utah.) Later he moved to Hammond, New Mexico and died in 1930 in the home of his son John Rush Norton in Eagar, being eighty-eight years old.[4]

According to a LDS manuscript history of Greer Ward:

> There were a few non-Mormon settlers in Lee's Valley at an early date before the saints thought of locating a settlement there, but in 1879 Peter Jens Jensen, Lehi Smithson, James Hale and Heber Dalton, with their families, and Richard Lee and sons took up claims at different points in the little valley lying along the upper Little Colorado river which subsequently became known as Lee's Valley. They built several cabins that year. When Ellis Whitney Wiltbank [patriarch and later bishop of the Greer Ward] visited the place in the summer of 1879 he found the families mentioned above living there and he remembers that Brother Peter Jens Jensen had a fine garden, and a good crop of grain growing. These first settlers attended meetings in

> Round Valley .... There was no church organization in Lee's Valley until 1896. The settlement so far has not been much of a success.[5]

James Hale, a widower, came into the valley with five sons, Isiah (Ike), Howard, Sam, Michal, Sylvester, and one daughter, Roxena. Not long before, his wife Elizabeth had become ill, died, and had been buried in Forest Dale. Forest Dale was then a settlement of about eleven Mormon families who built and farmed on what was later declared to be reservation land. Most families left by 1879-80, but the last were ordered off by the army in 1883 after wrathful Indians had come to plant crops and found white families still there.[6]

Hale's son, Sylvester, in a letter wrote of first locating (in Lee Valley) in old Father Jensen's home who, he says, had lived there and left before they came through. Of the hardships, Sylvester Hale speaks of his father's family and the Smithsons being the only ones left in the valley during the early years:

> It was during this time that Geronimo was raiding the country. These two families spent a great deal of time together because they were afraid of the Indians. They were almost afraid to sleep in the house for fear the Indians would set them on fire while they were in them .... There were very few crops raised at that time. The climate was higher and the seasons shorter than at the present. In the wintertime people weren't able to stay in Greer because of the deep snow and severe cold.[7]

It wasn't unusual for new families to move into others' one or two room cabins or dugouts. If they were seriously intending to locate, the "purchase" was made without money changing hands. Payments were made by trading parcels of land, teams, wagons, harness, etc. Mrs. Cleve Wiltbank spoke of acquiring the Howell property (in the early 1920s)—twenty-seven acres with a little house built by S. R. Howell in 1892—for $950 worth of horses and cattle.[8]

These early communities were very short of cash and transactions were mainly by barter. A man who worked for Gustav Becker as a fifteen-year-old, William B. Thompson, recalled he would help people find their goods—

> [The clerks] never knew the price of anything because everything was barter, except with tourists. The family would come in by wagon, come in the store and set out

sacks of grain, shingles, whatever; and put it in a pile in the middle of the floor. Then they'd show Gus Becker what they wanted to 'buy.' The old man and Becker would then go off into the office and see what deal they could make.[9]

Though farmers often didn't produce any extra, they were carried not only by Becker's but also by the old ACMI (Arizona Cooperative Mercantile Institution) in Eagar, a Mormon institution, the first of which were owned and operated by their stockholders—a kind of church counterpart to the Gentile mercantile-quasi-banking concerns which held the life strings of their creditors. In addition to "paying" by freighting, sometimes men and boys were called off by the church to work on irrigation systems, dams, ditches, and reservoirs in neighboring towns—being paid partly in wages, perhaps part withheld for a debt owed the ACMI or for a tithe.

Peterson, in writing of the Little Colorado River colonizers in Greer and Nutrioso, spoke of their poverty which he thought was more severe than that of other Little Colorado towns. Factors he cited for this poverty were being off the beaten path of church visitations; receiving little, perhaps nothing in the way of church subsidies; being isolated from communication, railroads; having to contend with geography and attendant severe weather which brought unseasonable freezes—killing crops and livestock.[10]

An old-timer, Mae Wiltbank (daughter of Sylvester Hale), spoke of her maternal grandfather Jacob Noah Butler who came in the 1890s with his two wives, Sarah and Sena, nineteen children, and located about one-quarter mile up Butler Canyon. There he built a little cabin with a large common room, a kitchen, and two bedrooms, one for "each family."

> They were so poor they never had anything .... They were so congenial you wouldn't know which kid belonged to which wife .... They lived on nothing; they didn't have nothing. Everybody was poor and they didn't know it.[11]

E. R. DeWitt first brought cows and oxen to pasture in Lee Valley in 1881 and spoke of people beginning to raise crops of oats, barley, potatoes, and a large variety of garden vegetables. The season was too short for fruit, although ninety-eight years later four gnarled apple trees still bloomed at the old Norton place. Great wagon expeditions went out in late summer and fall to gather wild thorny gooseberries and raspberries for the winter's jams and jellies. The "jars" for fruit products were often transformed from pint liquor bottles, cracked to the right size by burning a string tied around the bottles that had been dipped in coal oil.[12]

In the early 1880s as the range around Lee Valley was being stocked with cattle, and as there were no fences even separating the reservation, the range wars began—lasting well into the days of the Forest Reserve in the early 1900s. Beside the traditional feud over territories between the sheep and cattlemen, the rustlers with their trumped-up claims moved in. Even "honest folk" would gather in stray and wild cattle, horses and make domestics of them. The Indians would often steal across the "line" and take Anglos' cattle and horses to White River Agency, charging the cattlemen a grazing fee on them which would run from one to two dollars per head—considerable money then.[13]

James Hale was shot on Christmas Day, 1886 on the streets of Springerville. He and Lehi Smithson had been working for the old Twenty-Four and caught rustlers—the Clantons it is thought—having already stolen two herds and in the process of taking the third. Hale and Smithson reported them to the cattle company, and Smith and Carson got their cattle back. The rustlers, however, had it in for Hale after that and later, meeting up with him in town, finally proved that indeed a "bullet would go through a Mormon" (an excuse they offered over Hale's body). Some sources say the Westbrooks, remnants of the Butch Cassidy gang, were responsible for the murder.[14]

The huge cattle outfits brought some more positive impressions too. Judge Crosby recalled the roundups in the days of the old cattle kings:

> Each cowboy had a mount of from six to ten horses, and these were cared for by one or two of the men who were known as the wranglers. There were two or three wagons with the roundup, with a cupboard in the back of the wagon, and the cook usually drove the wagon from camp ground to camp ground with the front of the wagon filled with bed rolls. Reaching camp, the cook took no time to unhitch the horses, and someone else cut the wood for him. The cook was the first man up in the morning and the last one to bed at night. He would bake bread and fry beef in six Dutch ovens running all at the same time. Soda bread, beefsteak and coffee, with now and then some syrup or potatoes, supplied the food. There were usually two roundups a year—one in the summer for branding the calves and one in the fall for gathering the steers. If the rains were late, the two were often combined in the late summer or early fall. How those punchers did work during roundup time! As soon as it was daylight, they were off to ride the range and bring in all of the cattle, often as many as a thousand head, to a designated gathering ground. Then followed the branding of calves, sometimes way into the night, with the cutting back of the cattle that were to be left, the caring for the day herd of steers or cattle that were to be

taken to other ranges. Nothing in the West's industrial life ever appealed more to a full-red-blooded American boy than life on a cattle ranch.[15]

Communication between Lee Valley and the outside world grew as its lifeline sister towns established closer and faster sources of supply and mail. Though roads between towns continued to be rough in dry weather—with rocks that had to be thrown out as one went, with ruts, and in wet weather, bogs and occasionally quicksand—freighting by the mountain farmers continued between Springerville, St. Johns, Holbrook, and Fort Apache. Many times they were given black powder, caps and fuse in order to blow the heavy rocks out of the way—those which could not be handled by hand, or by pick and shovel, or crow bar.

Luckily Fort Apache had an insatiable appetite for fresh produce, grain, meat, and goods of every kind. As far as providing its own "mass transportation," the fort claimed the fastest thing around: The United States Army Ambulance or Coach went between Fort Apache and Holbrook, always pulled by a six mule team, to pick up important officials, military items, registered mail or packages, and the monthly payroll. Toward the end of the 1800s the military cut a road across the White and Black Rivers, linking the fort with the San Carlos Indian Reservation. This route eventually was extended to Globe. By 1895 the Beckers used horses and mules rather than oxen and most freighting between Springerville and New Mexico was to Magdalena, the end of the branch railroad line out of Socorro—a round trip of about eighteen days.

Mail was then brought along the Holbrook-St. Johns route by buckboard and from St. Johns by two wheel cart into Springerville, and later to Eagar. For many years the David K. Udall family had the mail contract. Through the mails came the catalogues of Montgomery Ward, Sears Roebuck and Company—Many gadgets and necessities were ordered from their pages.[16]

Meanwhile business in Springerville and other Little Colorado towns began to flourish. Lorenzo Hubbell, St. Johns, had a mail, passenger, and express line between Navajo, St. Johns, and Springerville; Solomon Barth, E. S. Stover, Colomo & Co., and A. Gonzales were purveyors in St. Johns in 1884—advertising in the newspaper staples, "tobacos," hats, caps, boots, "underware," Queensware (the blue-on-white glazed earthenware out of England), and stating they would pay the highest price for wool pelts, hides, and "live Stock." E. S. Stover, general merchandiser, in such an ad exhorted customers to "Keep on hand a large supply of wines, liquors, cigars, beer." There is little indication that many of the early settlers were caught short in those lines.

From a log of transactions at Becker Mercantile (calling itself the third oldest store in Arizona) during 1882, carefully written in script—ordered of John Becker, Belen, New Mexico:

60 Scks Rose of Kansas	at	$ .25	$255.00
6 plow handles right and left small		.24	1.44
1 Sett Thimbles and skeins			4.04
3 pounds rosin		.08	.24
3 Mat Cinnamon 12 pounds		.26	3.12
5 Gll Lard Oil		1.28	6.40
2 cases concentrated lye		1.24	9.92
1 dz. brooms			4.05
3 Dz Blck Spool Thread		.57& ⅔	1.74
6 Coils Galv barbed wire		.12	78.36
4 Looking Glasses 14x24		1.40	5.69
1 Pound Sulphur			.11
½ Pound Cloroform		2.00	1.00
1 Bx. Cig. Paper			1.06
3 Winchester Rifles 46-60		17.47	52.41
1 Gross Wine Corks			.54
⅓ Lemon Extract		4.70	1.57
10 Boxes Adams Chewing Gum		10.40[?]	4.00
1 [?] Prunes			3.75
2 Kegs Syrup		2.60	5.20
½ Pound Ess. of Peppermint		1.00	.50
1/6 Woole Cards		3.18	.53
1/6 Shaving Brushes		.70	.12
1 No 8 Cook Stove			22.95
95 Pounds Horseshoes No 1 & 2			7.70
10 Pounds Long Cut Durham		.83 & ⅓	8.84
46 ½ Gll Jmp Burbon		1.00	46.50

Also on the books, listing orders and amounts owed were those by some of Lee Valley's first residents: Peter Jensen, Lehi Smithson, James Hale, Heber Dalton, Richard Lee, John Norton, Thomas Lang (from 1879-81) ordering everything from tallow, barley, shingles, bacon, tea, soda, nails, tobacco, candlewick, matches, ladies' shoes (at $1.50), to thread, shirting, rice, sugar, and whiskey.[17]

One necessity which was shipped in from New Mexico was salt and Becker's early letter and billing head shows they were, among other things, "dealers in salt." It came from the Salt Lake, west of Magdalena, near the state border, and much of it was used for brine—so vital to the pioneer in preserving food. Settlers spoke of stopping en route to Springerville, washing and sacking the salt for later use. At that time the Beckers were also augmenting the pioneers' typical diet of wild game by selling native Apache trout taken out of what was to be one of the oldest manmade fishing lakes in Arizona—more recently called "Becker Lake." The lake was completed in 1880, and in it native fish grew to such an amazing size, Gustav Becker decided to sell the "yellow-bellies" each Tuesday and Friday.

> [He selected those that had] reached a length that the heads and tails reached above the rim of the large dishpans in which they were displayed. As the pans were at least sixteen inches in diameter, many of the trout were over twenty-four inches in length.[18]

The people around Lee Valley subsisted almost entirely on deer, elk, antelope, turkey, and occasionally bear, squirrel, rabbit—perhaps once a year, in the wintertime when it could be kept, beef. (In desperate straights a porcupine might even make a meal.) People mostly "fished" for fish—But on one occasion Roy Hall (son of John Oscar and Lucy Hall who homesteaded on Hall Creek in about 1894) caught his mother's prize rooster, just purchased from Aunt Nan Lund, at the end of his brother's fishing pole which had been tossed on top the house. Roy threw the line to the rooster who gobbled up the grasshopper in one gulp—The family had a delicious (and of anonymous origin) chicken dinner that evening.[19]

What later became known as the "Greer Lakes" began as reservoirs for irrigation in Round Valley. The three lakes were "Bunch," with about 512 acre feet capacity, date of appropriation, 1887, holding third filling right on the Little Colorado River; "Tunnel," same date of filling right with 694 acre feet storage; "River or No. 3," sixth right, date of appropriation, 1896, 1,669 acre feet capacity. A ditch was dug to take water out of the Little Colorado River in the village proper. It went around the western perimeter of the valley, north of the village, feeding "Bunch" and "Tunnel." The river itself filled "River Reservoir." Water was then carried in the stream until Bigelow Crossing, where some was taken by ditch to what was then "Amity." The ditches and lakes are still part of the Round Valley Water Users Association.

According to the Eagar Ward dedicatory booklet:

> These reservoirs and canals were laid out without surveying instruments. They were built largely by hand, having no blasting powder, and when large rocks were encountered they were removed by building fires on them and broken up by dashing cold water on them. . . . The first dynamite ever seen here by the oldtimers was used by [the] Hale brothers in blasting Tunnel Reservoir. Tunneling from both ends without surveying instruments, this tunnel met almost perfectly.[20]

More families moved into Lee Valley after 1890, and it began to take on a different aspect. E. R. DeWitt, having recently married A. V. Greer's daughter, Willmirth, took up a homestead east of River Reservoir. They shared quarters with another Greer daughter Susan Virginia, married to Duane Hamblin. (Duane Hamblin was a son of William, brother of Jacob.) On the DeWitt homestead in 1893, 330 bushels of oats, 26 tons of oat hay off 12 acres, and 30,000 pounds of potatoes from 3 acres were raised. The DeWitts were the first to have the threshers—the thresher's toll being paid in grain.[21]

Others that came in were the James McDaniel family; John Black family; Samuel H. Howell family; Richard and Joe Bleak and families; a Gibson family; and Henry P. Hobson. The Howell home (later to be called the oldest standing structure in Greer) was two rooms of rough lumber. Later occupants, the Cleve Wiltbanks, added a log portion to the north. From a Howell family "affair" evolved the names of nearby "Benny" and "Rosey" Creeks.[22]

Sometime prior to 1892, Ellis Whitney Wiltbank and John Black had started a water-powered sawmill, taking logs from the valley, largely cleared by those early loggers and farmers who needed the land for crops. The mill was located about where the old Cliff Wentz garage later was—the water taken by ditch or race from the river three-quarters of a mile to the southeast, and brought up a flume, dropping on to the wooden wheel. Later his wife (Wiltbank's) had an 8x10-foot cheese house built over the ditch so that her cheeses could be kept at a constant, cool temperature.

Ellis Whitney and his wife Hannah Mary Hall Wiltbank moved their family to Lee Valley in about 1894. The family grew to include William Ellis (father of Atella Haws and Milo Wiltbank); Mary Ann ("Aunt Mollie" [Crosby, later Butler]); Florence (married to John C. Hall); Ida (married to Willis S. Gibbons); Hyrum (married to Sadie Burk); John Cleveland (married to Afton Haws); Milford J. (married to Geneva Plumb); Rebecca (married to Minor Leroy Hall, later William J. Burgess); and Josephine (born in Greer in 1897—married to Roland S. Hamblin). Most of Wiltbanks' children, and later their husbands and wives, spent considerable time in Lee Valley in various capacities through the years.

By 1896 the area's first school house, 30x20 feet, was built of sawed logs, having a lumber floor and shingle roof. (Shingles, as well as adobe were being made by Jacob Butler. He had a shingle mill southwest of the settlement and made adobe in Butler Canyon.) The first classes, consisting of 25-30 children, were taught by Sister Emma Coleman for three months during the summer of 1897—the children then going to Eagar for the remainder of the winter. The teacher lived in a room on the back of the school house. During the first years, school was taught from a chart and the children sat on plain, rough benches.

Lunch was always brought by the child, and typically consisted of sourdough biscuits and pork, beef, or cheese in between. If the family was large, the bread might be put in a ten-pound bucket, then partly filled with milk. If the weather was cold, the children of that family would set it on the stove to warm. Then at noon, one might see two to six children eating from the bucket. Water was brought in daily in a bucket and each used a common dipper for drinking.[23]

Who and when they attended was flexible—the only rule being that the child be smaller than the teacher so as not to cause much trouble. The boys were often off with the harvest or cattle and if the parents didn't have anything else for them to do, they were sent to school. The first high school in the county, St. Johns Academy, wasn't founded until 1889, and many a boy, as a man, was taught by his wife to read and write.

One of the most important stabilizing events in Lee Valley's growth was being organized as a branch of the LDS church. In 1896 E. W. Wiltbank served as presiding elder; Elijah R. DeWitt, branch clerk; Jacob Noah Butler, choir leader. Wiltbank was then made bishop and Greer became a full ward in 1897—Elijah R. DeWitt, James McDaniel, Dan H. Wright, and W. S. Gibbons were named as counselors. Ellis Whitney was

Home of Ellis Whitney Wiltbanks'

The Tithing House

to devote some thirteen years to the ward. He was reputed to be so religious that before the community had a church, he would walk to Sunday school in Eagar because he didn't want his horses to work on the Sabbath. When the first church was still smoldering from a fire in 1900, he had wood on the spot, ready to start rebuilding the next morning.[24]

Sometime after, a tithing office was built south of the present Crosby Store and the Mormons followed their custom of paying one-tenth of their increase into the church. Since it was difficult in the early days to obtain money, tithing was paid in kind, out of whatever they had—eggs, hay, pigs, grain, lumber—and stored by the bishop until he could convert the goods to money and forward to church headquarters.

On December 9, 1896, Mollie Wiltbank married Lorenzo Crosby. Later in a double ceremony with her brother, William Ellis, who had married "Ren's" sister, Sarah Amelia Crosby, the couples solemnized their vows by taking the honeymoon trail to the temple at St. George, Utah—traveling twenty-one days to get there and sharing along the way a special treat, a case of salmon.[25]

Lee Valley changed its name to "Greer" about this time. (Some say this was requested because "Lee Valley" was too long for the postmark.) In a tape recording before her death, Willmirth Greer DeWitt said that Bishop George H. Crosby of Eagar called a meeting asking those present to suggest names for the area. Bishop Crosby suggested they name it after "a good old man," A. V. Greer, and that was agreed upon.[26]

The next boost was getting a post office. E. W. Wiltbank applied but his wife, Hannah Mary, was named postmaster by President William J. McKinley because she was a Republican. She operated the post office out of her home as was the custom until Mrs. George E. Crosby (P.M. 1959-71) had it in a separate building. From the *St. Johns Herald*, April 9, 1898:

> A new post office has been established at Greer precinct, Apache County, with Mrs. Hannah M. Wiltbank as postmistress. As some of our readers may not know where Greer is—and we have heard the inquiry repeatedly made as to its location—we would say that Greer precinct is what was formerly known as "Lee Valley." The locality has been re-christened in honor of the late A. V. Greer, Esq., who was a pioneer and prominent citizen of the southern part of this county. The location of Greer settlement is in one of the most beautiful valleys in the country, rivaling any of the nooks and corners of the Adirondacks, of New York. If at-

tractive surroundings, beautiful scenery, and pleasant neighbors count for anything, Greer precinct will become quite a large village.

The first mail contract was let to S. R. Howell, being carried on horseback twice a week and paying $200 per year. Some eighty years later, his daughter Sally Howell Brown recalled riding with her father in a two-wheel cart, drawn by one horse.[27]

As men wrested a living from the soil, from shingle and lumber mills, freighting, and occasional road work which was often done "for free" to pay off the small annual road tax of one or two dollars assessed by the county—women worked long and hard to support the family in other ways. During the summers the butter and cheeses they made were an important item in the "budget." They would take these to places like Concho in the fall to trade for fresh fruit and molasses. Some of the dairy products were kept for the family during the winter. In the late 1800s, cheese brought 12-15 cents per pound and butter, 25 cents per pound.[28]

The cheese was made in a big vat into which the evening's milk would be strained. In the morning, the morning's milk would be added. Some twenty or thirty range cattle might be milked to get enough for the "batch." The milk was heated on the wood stove to a certain temperature, cheese coloring and rennet (enzymes from lining of calf's stomach) were added. The mixture was kept at an even temperature for an hour, setting into curds and whey. Cutting into small curds and taking off all the whey took about four hours. Then it was cooled, salt added, and put in a press. After twenty-four hours the cheese, which might weigh eight pounds, was put on a shelf, turned every day to prevent mold, and any cracks rubbed with butter. After being cured for two months, it was ready.

During the 1900s, several families made it a custom to go up on the mountain, to Slade Ranch or "Milk Ranch" (near Sunrise Lake), during the summer so their cows could get better grass. They would then make their cheese up there.[29]

Effie May Butler Wiltbank, daughter of Jacob Butler (married to George Wiltbank in 1912), in her manuscript sketch of life in "our canyon home in Greer," told of customs during her childhood around the turn of the century: Barrels were used to catch rain; to make soap, leaching lye from ashes; for vinegar, adding any bit of sweetened water; to store meat, either wild or beef; and to put brine into for storing butchered pigs. The five-gallon cans kerosene came in were used to bring water from the stream, for cooking, washing, bean cooking, etc.

She spoke of her father's .45-.70 caliber gun and remembered him pouring molten lead into a bullet mold. Caps and powder had to be bought and were very precious—and matches, scarce.

Kerosene lights were considered a luxury. For many the lighting system consisted of candles or even a "bitch light," made by braiding cotton string, putting this string into a small vessel containing grease, lighting the end and "my what a smell!" Mrs. Wiltbank also recalled the use of pitch torches, held in the bedroom while babies were tucked in!

Wooden tubs were necessities, but temperamental, as they had to be kept damp or they would fall to pieces. Wash day would find two tubs set side by side on a long bench with a wash board handy. The clothes were run through several scrubbings; then boiled in a five gallon can on the stove; then rubbed on the board; then rinsed through two waters—one clear, one of bluing—then spread on the bushes in the summer, and on the snow in the winter.

Contents of the early medicine chest were mostly harvested from around springs, rivers, and hillsides. Herbs were gathered and hung from ceiling and wall to dry—hops, horsemint, peppermint, yarrow, wild grape root, quaking aspen bark, raspberry leaves. Hops were steeped for nerves; yarrow for cramps; horsemint combined with other "stuff," and boiled for canker medicine; sulfur, cream of tartar and sugar made "stuff" for purifying the blood. Grape root and aspen bark tea were also combined with sulfur and molasses in the spring of the year to cleanse the blood of impurities. Yarrow, steeped in milk, cured coughs; senna leaves were a laxative; and mustard plasters invaluable for localized aches and deep chest colds. Liniment was a "must" and one way they made it was to buy some camphor, put it in a pretty bottle, then steep it in liquor.[30]

Through the J. Ling catalogue one could get cheap perfumes, beads, and trinkets. The rest of the outfitting, however, was mostly home-made—often cut from newspaper patterns fashioned after pictures in Sears Roebuck catalogues.

Girls never wore pants, but for everyday had dark dresses with long sleeves and high necks. The petticoats were of flour-sacking (or "factory," like muslin; or in winter, of outing flannel or gray knit), with one "nice," of cambric. Under this was a chemis and a sleeveless "panty waist" that had buttons on it for buttoning underpants to; and knitted stockings (later black stockings), which before elastic, were rigged to the buttons with string.

Women always wore dresses below the ankles, with aprons they put on as they got up in the morning. For Sunday they might have black flared, or gathered skirts with white "waists," a belt, and a nice pair of buttoned shoes, "if you were lucky." A girl's nice dress might be of calico or occasionally, wool—although the latter would seldom be worn as it couldn't be washed. Wraps consisted of shawls and capes, with accessories: muffs, hats, and knitted "fascinators"—a type of scarf for the head with ends that wrapped around the neck.

Boys often didn't graduate to pants until they were several years old. Mae Hale Wiltbank remembered her brother of about six, immaculate in a white dress, returning very muddied after gathering eggs. Older boys wore overalls, as men did; "little old coats;" perhaps knickerbockers for nice that came just below the knees; with knitted caps or "Huckleberry Finn" straw hats.

Shoes were a precious commodity—especially in large families. A pair of shoes was supposed to last a year and by spring had been patched and resoled. From April to September the kids went barefoot and as a pioneer said, left many "toenails all over those mountains"![31]

One of the hottest arguments between oldtimers occurred over just how many miles an individual had danced as opposed to another. From 1880 on, dances were a favorite recreation both in Round Valley and Greer. At first few, if any non-Mormons were admitted. The Clantons showed up at one Amity dance with hats, chaps, spurs, and pistols—saying they were really going to howl. They were given "the boot" and told to howl outside. Remembered Mollie Butler: "The dances were very orderly . . . . and supervised by a floor manager who watched the young people carefully, and if they didn't dance as they should, he stopped the music and instructed them how to dance properly."[32]

At first only square dances were done and the boy was not permitted to put his arm around the girl. "Round dances" (Schottische, waltz, polka, Chicago glide, two-step), were considered "real bad." Willmirth Greer DeWitt remembered at conference time the priesthood taking up the matter of round dances. The leaders decided the saints could have two "round dances" an evening. They were soon acceptable, however, and then the "mileage" began to mount up in earnest. Music was played by both friends and relatives, men and women—on the piano, violin, harp, organ, and guitar—some dancing and playing at the same time.[33]

Harvest time was also a celebration. Potato harvest was almost like a picnic remembered Mollie Butler. Everybody helped, they ate and sang, and potatoes were hauled out of Greer by wagon-loads. Also threshing time was an event. When the thresher first came to Greer in about 1896, the grain was cut with sickles and scythes, then cradled or bundled, shocked, stacked in conical piles, waiting for equipment and crews.

Threshing Time

The thresher—horse powered—would come over the mountains from Eagar or Nutrioso. Sometimes the apparatus would have to be weighted with logs so it wouldn't slide, with horses to the rear for additional "braking" as it was pulled by team down the steep incline into Greer. Five teams of horses would be used to turn the tumbling rod that turned the machinery. A six-man crew came with the thresher, but sixteen to eighteen men helped. It meant a lot of cooking for the farmer's wife and it was one of the few occasions for which a beef was butchered. The best linen was brought out —"Nothing was too good for them," according to Effie May Wiltbank.[34]

On one occasion, recalled Irl Lund, his dad Marion was looking for a missing heifer who disappeared at threshing time and never did find her. The next spring she emerged from the straw pile alive, but a little thinner. 'Seems in the fall she somehow climbed up on an adjacent building; had fallen through the straw pile; wintered between the pile and the building, drinking the melting snow that seeped through; and literally ate her way out in the spring![35]

In a letter of January 15, 1937 to John Butler regarding those early days, E. R. DeWitt wrote:

> Well, I just tell you these things to show how we lived in those days; we all farmed, had cattle and sheep and made butter and cheese, worked for wages, freighted, run in debt, but always paid; fished and hunted and were always happy and never paid a license. If anything I have wrote will do you any good I am well paid; if it don't help you any I have lost nothing.

47

On The Road To Nowhere

1924 Dodge
"A good old mountain car"

IV

Strangers In Town

"'Guess with a school, a Sunday school, a new name, and a post office, you'd say we were living in town, so to speak," wrote an early Greer resident.[1]

"Oh, it was hard, but we didn't know it was hard because we didn't know anything different," added another voice from the past.[2]

People would gather for church, dances, and entertainments, and have at least one potluck meal together each week—all of which helped soften the edges of the "hardness." If one looked around, he stood about eye level with the fellow down the valley, across the meadow.

Townspeople would come from all around in their wagons to dances at the school house. They'd bring supper and quilts; eat and bed down the children on the benches; dance until midnight, eat again; dance until daylight; then put everyone in the wagon and go home. Holidays were celebrated together, too, with a community Christmas tree at the school house. They didn't have much in the way of gifts—a stocking with an orange, an apple, perhaps some candy, and handmade toys like willow whistles. But there was always a Santa Claus, dressed in regulation

49

red—although he could usually be identified by "the stripe" of his work socks. One year a proud father slipped his newborn son under the tree as an added attraction.

On the Fourth of July remembered John Hamblin,

> ... At dawn father always got up, took his 30-30 rifle off the wall, stepped outside and emptied the magazine into the air. His shots would echo from one mountain across the valley to another [valley] ... and as soon as father's shots had died away, another rancher would take up the barrage, and that was the way the celebration started.[3]

Later on in the morning at the school grounds, patriotic songs would be followed by someone in an Uncle Sam outfit giving a "stump speech." The program was punctuated by volleys of fire let loose on signal by riflemen stationed nearby. After the program there was a potluck picnic with races, games, and lemonade. Reminisced Hamblin, "... I [later] remembered the early days in Greer, when the celebration was just for the sheer joy of it, and everything was free."[4]

There would be few crossing the foot bridge over the Little Colorado on their way into town who couldn't hail at least five around as cousin, either kissing or shirt-tail; and most would be closer relations. Blood lines formed a strong, self-sufficient, self-perpetuating system that brought nourishment and support in the remote village where reality was often harsh. Even though it had become known for a "Post Office, Greer Precinct," the natives were still years away from seeing many strangers in town.

Some of the settlers of the late 1800s left Greer at the turn of the century, but brothers and sisters, sons and daughters, uncles and aunts, cousins came to take up their places.

"Around the hill," northwest of the village proper, moved John C. Hall, married to Florence Wiltbank. Her uncles, George and Frank (brothers of Ellis Whitney Wiltbank), homesteaded land beneath Amberion Point; later setting up bachelors' quarters at the Hall place in Greer—The Halls took as trade the Wiltbank brothers' place in Eagar. Another sister of E.W.W., Nan, having a hand for carpentry, largely built the two-room house in which she and her husband, William W. Lund, lived below the old school house. Fifteen years later their son, Marion, began and raised his family on the same site.

The Haws came to live on the old Norton place about 1910. By then "the place" had been acquired by Pete Peterson of St. Johns and run as part of his sheep outfit. He brought his sister, Dorthea Haws (a widow), and eight of her twelve children to live at the ranch. Mrs. Haws later married one of the bachelors, Frank Wiltbank, in 1914; her daughter Afton married his nephew, John Cleveland Wiltbank, in 1919.

Another Wiltbank, Mollie Wiltbank Crosby, moved back to Greer in about 1902 with three children, while her husband Lorenzo was on a LDS mission. The Crosbys had homesteaded on a beautiful, but lonely piece of land on the east fork of Black River at what was later known as "Crosby Crossing," where they lived for part of six years. During that time they operated a little store there, raised crops, and ran cattle. An old photo showed a covered wagon approaching the Crosbys' log ranch house—the land bordered by ripgut fence (criss-crossed logs), widely used by Little Colorado settlers. Their first child, Hannah, was born in Eagar, 1898; their second, George Ellis, on the east fork ranch, 1900; and Lester Lorenzo in Greer, 1902. Their father (Lorenzo) was shot in his berth on a train in Missouri while returning from his mission, 1904. Some thought he was killed by members of the Smith gang (originally from Missouri) with whom he had trouble on the east fork ranch; others thought the fatal wound was self-inflicted.

Despite hardship and tragedy, "The settlers of Greer [were] a hardy people. Born and reared at [that] great altitude, they [were] men and women and children of more than average height, and of tremendous lung expansion," opined James Willard Schultz.[5]

"It's because we ate lots of rutabagas that had lots of that vitamin in 'em that's real good for you," said another.[6]

Nonetheless, accidents with axes, saws, and farm equipment took their toll in fingers and mangled limbs; as well as burns from scalding liquids (used among other things, to dip the hogs in before scraping off the bristle and butchering); and kerosene fires, etc. When illness came, such as the epidemic of scarlet fever in the early 1900s, little could be done but quarantine the families. Three children died from the disease during the winter of 1909—Lorenzo Crosby, Mary Lund, and Jay Hale. A cousin of one of them remembered stories of the children having to be lowered into their graves by a parent or close relative for fear the germs would spread.

Childbirth was usually assisted by a midwife. Before cars, and especially during the winter, the midwife might come several weeks to a month in advance and move in with the "expecting family." One midwife, Aunt Cele Hamblin ". . . would come and maybe wait for a month. I remember she'd make salt rising bread, [while she waited] . . . Worst smelling stuff on earth, but it tasted delicious," Mae Wiltbank remembered of times her brothers and sisters were born in Greer.[7]

51

"I didn't think anyone was a native of Greer—I thought everyone was born in our home in Eagar. I remember we had a bedroom that they'd come to when 'it was time,' and Mom would help them," said Buzz Haws of his mother, Atella.[8]

A granddaughter of E. W. Wiltbank, Mrs. Haws was a registered nurse with a (state-required) certificate as midwife. As far as the state was concerned, to be licensed as midwife in the 1920s required no examination or knowledge at all she remembered—just a certificate. She was equipped with cord-tie and silver nitrate for the babies' eyes—No anesthetic was used although she carried chloroform; and no surgical techniques used, though she said they were often needed.[9]

After the Forest Service strung the telephone wire into the ranger station in Greer, the doctor in Springerville or Eagar (when there was one) could be called. When he came with his awful "horsehair stitches," he wouldn't want to wait around—so several last-minute callers ended up delivering without his help. During one winter's snow storm, a family's best horse was used to pull the doctor's car from the Greer cutoff into town for a local delivery. The horse was never much good after that. There was no hospital for miles until Springerville opened one in 1936.

In addition to the rigors occurring as a matter of course in the pioneers' lives, came those imposed by the creation of the Black Mesa Forest Reserve by order of President William McKinley in 1898. By 1908 the reserve had been divided into two sections and the names changed: To the south, "Apache National Forest" which included Greer, Springerville, Blue River, and Clifton; and to the north, "Sitgreaves National Forest." Jurisdiction for the forests also changed from the Department of Interior to the Department of Agriculture—and the United States Forest Service was created.

What had all gone for free before: grazing, timber, water, land, were put under close scrutiny and a fee system—and people winced, sweated, sneered, and tried ways to escape the new stiff collar of restrictions and bureaucracy. The few supporters of the reserve idea (Gustav Becker was one, according to Fred Winn, supervisor of Apache National Forest, 1914-18.) found ". . . the conservation idea [hard to defend] among a people who were as a rule, hostile to the entire theory and in addition who for generations had been bred to the doctrine of laissez-faire."[10]

By 1911 the USFS had on the Apache National Forest 22,000 head of cattle and horses under permit, grazing under 200 different allotments; 52,000 head of sheep in 20 different permits; 1,240 goats and 133 head of hogs. It also employed a hunter and trapper at the supervisor's headquarters in Springerville to help exterminate predators of the livestock—bears, lions, wolves, bobcats, and coyotes. During the year ending

June, 1910 the Forest Service also sold in Apache National Forest 2,709,000 feet of timber and under its "free use regulation," gave 920,566 board feet to local settlers and ranchers for improvement of their homes and ranches.[11]

Teddy Roosevelt called for men "with bark on," but many of the supervisors and rangers trying to interpret and administer the regulations were from the East—thin-skinned, green—and appalled by the lack of amenities, not to mention the absence of any "real" roads through the forest, telephones, telegraphs, etc., and the administration of law by rifle or six-shooter. Some of the better men were those who either quickly gave up their spit and polish or those who were taken off the range and brought into the service.

At first (1905-06) the "uniform" of the forest ranger blended in with the terrain: Levi Strauss, work shirt, short blue denim jacket, and a wide-brimmed Stetson; often augmented with chaps, gun belt, and six-shooter. Later (1908-17), it was described as the "German crown prince uniform," which was said to also resemble in design and color what was then being worn by bellhops in certain hotels. By 1918, the design had come into the "English army officer period," with open collars and large bellows pants.[12]

The rangers supervised three areas: grazing, fire patrol, and timbering. For the first time, the cattlemen had to pay to graze their cattle on the forest and were confined to a given territory. What little cash they made from selling cattle went to pay taxes and grazing fees recalled some early permittees. Cattle rustling, according to an early account, went on unabated:

> Only when a friendless chap got caught was he taken to court. Most cases were settled on the ground, at the time, and many times one man was left on the ground when the case was closed.[13]

Some rangers also thought the forest was being overrun by unpermitted horses. In the 1920s Ranger Jess Fears said he gathered up 2,600 (unpermitted) head on the Greer district.[14]

In spite of ranges for sheep and cattle being officially "separate," cattlemen continued to complain about sheep crossing their territory. In the spring the sheep were driven from lower elevations to the White Mountains, sometimes taking two months for the drive, and foraging in a broad swath along the route. Finally, milewide driveways were established—designated routes along which the herds had to be driven at the rate of at least five miles per day.[15] On one such driveway, going from the

Forest Ranger Jim Siger,
Apache National Forest
ca. 1910

Green's Peak Lookout
ca. 1915

South Fork near Eagar, up on the mountain through Joe Baca Draw, were aspen carved with names of Spanish sheepdrivers, with dates in the early 1900s.

Poor communication and lack of equipment were particular problems in fire fighting. The first tools used by rangers were the ax, shovel, and mattock, and the gist of their instructions: Look for the fire and put it out. Usually that meant establishing a fire line and praying for rain. By about 1920 lookout towers and cabins were being built in the White Mountains—the towers constructed of poles—on Escudilla, Mount Baldy, Green's Peak, Pole Knoll; telephone lines strung from the towers to ranger stations; lookout people and fire fighters hired; and construction of fire patrol trails begun. In 1911 a Forest Service telephone line was strung between Water Canyon at the upper end of Eagar, mostly from tree to tree, for ten and one-half miles into the Greer ranger station.

Greer had been ranger headquarters since 1904, with David I. Penrod the first in residence. At that time the ranger had to cover the country from Vernon to Nutrioso and the work had to be done on horseback. Ranger H.O. Eaton constructed the Greer ranger station ("Riverside") in 1908. Eaton was followed by Rangers E. R. Patterson, Sizer, Wigley, Wylder, Billingslea, Swapp, DeCamp, Haynes, and Fears. After 1929 the station was only occupied seasonally. The most "famous" lookout persons locally were two young women who were hired during World War I to fill in for the men and were stationed at Mount Baldy: Hannah Crosby Kimball (in 1917) and Kathrine Anderson Fritz (in 1918).[16]

Finally, the timber stand was measured, its value estimated, and capacity as a watershed "officially" appreciated. In a letter of June 13, 1916 to the Secretary of Agriculture, Henry S. Graves, the Forester of the United States, wrote of Apache National Forest (especially the northern part):

> The timber stand is upward of one and three quarter billion feet and for the most part can be economically logged—of even more importance is the value of the area for water-shed protection. . . . [In this region] are found the headwaters of three of the four most important waters in Arizona—the Little Colorado, the Salt and the Gila, all of which are tributary to the fourth, the Colorado River. Among the important tributaries are the San Francisco, the Blue and the Black Rivers. . . .[17]

Logging no longer went on helter-skelter—Trees had to be marked and fees paid in advance of cutting. The industry grew with both small operators and larger outfits. The Whiting Brothers of St. Johns had been in the area since 1907, the year they leased their first mill in Milligan's

Valley. In 1912 they established a mill below Green's Peak which operated until 1943. Thirty-five miles from Greer, the new Apache Railway
Company from 1917-20 laid seventy-two miles of track between its new
sawmill at "Cluff Cienega" (later "Cooley") and Holbrook. In 1924 the W.
M. Cady Lumber Company of Louisiana purchased the mill and railroad
and changed the name of the mill site from "Cooley" to "McNary." In
February of that year, 411 passengers with black skins peered through the
windows of six coaches at equally curious whites, on their way to new jobs
in McNary—a long way from their Louisiana homes.[18]

Sawmilling locally lost Ellis Whitney Wiltbank who left Greer about
1908-10, having sold or given away most of his land and tried most every-
thing—the timber business, cattle and sheep, and farming. (The Greer
Ward had been discontinued in 1910.) He and his wife moved to St.
Johns where she ran a dormitory. Many relatives and children from all
over the countryside went there to live with them and go to St. John's
Academy (LDS), which had been the only high school for miles; although
Round Valley High was opened in 1921.

Timbering and processing were taken up at various sites during the
1900s—moving "where the trees were." Francis Day had a place on the
west fork road; Ike Issacson had a mill just outside Greer on the McNary
road; and east of River Reservoir, Fred Burk took over the ranch his parents, John S. and Melissa, had since about 1912, and started a mill
adjacent to what became in the twenties, a shingle mill owned by Henry
Day.

On another site in the 1930s, Burk was running a steam-operated
sawmill. As a teenager, Ed Dentzer Jr. remembered going up to Greer in
the summer where he and another local boy, Denzel Lund, would "sneak
down there at night, tie the whistle cord down, and run like heck—That
durn thing would blow and blow. 'Course he [Burk] was through for the
day, so it was just surplus steam, didn't hurt him. But it was sure effective for us."[19] Burk later used a car motor to run his saw.

One day in 1910, a fellow came through Springerville and opened a
new automobile route as well as a pandora's box full of new opportunities
for those Little Colorado communities not on the railroad line. Engaged
by the National Highway Association to find an ocean to ocean auto
route, A.L. Westgard followed a New Mexico sheepherder's directions
into Springerville arriving in his "Pathfinder." From there, Gustav
Becker recommended the government military route through Cooley,
Cooley's Ranch, Fort Apache, through San Carlos, Globe, to Yuma
—finally ending at Los Angeles. Westgard made two other trips, in a
Saurer truck and a Premier 6-60, during the next several years carrying
rolls of canvas and three planks, 3"x12"x16', to negotiate sand and mud.

Since there were no bridges over the White and Black Rivers, he got men on horseback to pull him across.

In the land-locked villages like Greer where women might only get to town two or three times a year—for LDS conference, Fourth of July, and perhaps to have a baby—the impact of Westgard's treks was not immediate. But the development of roads and courting the new "machines" became a life-long effort of Gustav Becker and later his son Julius, and in 1913 the first Ocean to Ocean Highway Convention was held in Springerville. As entertainment for the conventioneers, the first Round Valley Rodeo was held—on the main street of Springerville. Local cowboys as well as those from Nutrioso, Alpine, and Greer were the performers. The acknowledged "star" of the rodeo, however, was Roy Hall. With a broken leg, he won the $35 prize offered for staying on the worst horse in the country.[20]

In a letter of May 16, 1912 Gustav Becker wrote, "We have an auto line carrying mail from Holbrook, they make the trip in ten hours. They have Steamer Cars, and can carry nine people besides mail."[21] Becker also kept a log-book of early-day transcontinental automobile travel to help promote highways through the area. Beginning in 1912 (to 1919) famous cross-country racers signed in, E. G. (Cannonball) Baker and Barney Oldfield; as well as Edsel B. Ford and Lt. George S. Patton. *The* (Miami) *Arizona Silver Belt* (December 18, 1923) noted 15,000 "tourist machines" had passed through Springerville during the first ten months of 1923.

Starting the first auto dealership around, Becker sold four EMF'30 and Flanders automobiles in 1910. Since most travel up to that time was by Bain wagon, the ruts around the countryside were "wagon-wide," sixty inches. The span between tires in the new autos was fifty-six. Becker solved the dilemma by ordering four sets of sixty-inch axles and installing them on the new cars. From then on the only difficulty remaining were the deep ruts which wore out the sides of the tires rather than the tread.[22]

In a small brochure printed in 1915 by the Observer Printers, St. Johns, an appeal was made by the county, wanting—

> ... [a] desirable class of immigration to help develop its many resources. Land near Eagar can be bought for $40.00 to $150.00 per acre with perpetual water rights. It is estimated that there are at least ten turkey to every square mile in the county as well as grizzlies, cougars, etc.

> [In the same booklet Dr. T. J. Bouldin, Superintendent of Health, said] We have often wondered why people would persist in trying to live in a hot malarial district or a cold, unpleasant country when Northern Arizona can furnish all that is desirable for happiness and longevity.... That Apache County is one of the most healthful subdivisions of

our country can be proven and besides, the appearance of its people is a living testimonial to the effect.[23]

The first bona fide "tourist," not visiting "family," in Greer was James Willard Schultz, who didn't drive in but came on the railroad to Holbrook, and from there by wagon. By the time Schultz came to Greer he had begun a second career, writing tales of Indians in serialized magazine form, and in what were to total, thirty-seven books. His first "line" had been that of a Hudson Bay Co. trader among the Plains Indians dealing in buffalo hides and watered-down whiskey. Feeling himself to be a misfit in his wealthy New York family's regime, he escaped to the plains at eighteen. There he lived among the Blackfeet Indians, learning their language, marrying a young Pikuni, "Natahki," and following the buffalo herds as their dwindling numbers—brought on by the white man's fences, cattle, and sheep—presaged the end of that era for both Indian and trader. After the death of his wife, he wandered out to California on writing jobs, then to Arizona, working among Southwest Indians and excavating ruins at Casa Grande and the Tonto Valley near Roosevelt.[24]

Schultz built "Apuni Oyis" (Butterfly Lodge) across from the ranger station in 1913 and was remembered in Greer as acting more like an Indian than white—quiet, walking 300 yards ahead of his wife (his second) as they went for the mail, and distant from children (although many could barely wait for the next installment of one of his tales they were reading in *Boy's Life*).

Of more dramatic presence was his son, Hart ("Lone Wolf"), who stood about 6'6" and spent many seasons in Greer with his wife, Naomah. He would show up at community picnics in full Blackfoot regalia; and on one occasion when he had too much to drink, made a white friend dress in the buckskin outfit and "dance to the Indian," with Lone Wolf's six-shooter pointed at the compliant fellow's feet. One time a young mother was so worried about him drinking and galloping through the village vowing to kill all the Mormons, she stuffed her kids in a cupboard.

Mainly Lone Wolf was remembered as an artist of note who had turned down $5,000 for the painting he did of the Grand Canyon that hung over the fireplace at Schultz' Greer lodge. Many people visited the artist in his studio there—listening to Indian tales and of his struggle to become an artist and sculptor. He began as a child with "brushes of bone" to paint on stretched buckskin and as a young man, trained at the

"Apuni Oyis"
Home of James Willard Schultz & Lone Wolf

The Thompson's Lodge on the Hill

Art Institute in Chicago. Just above the fireplace opening, set into the face, was a relief of buffalo he did. The studio was jammed with memorabilia—his paintings, sculpture, old guns, many of his father's books. On the walls were hung his grandfather Yellow Wolf's suit (over one hundred years old) with hairs from the fifteen to twenty scalps of enemy Indians Yellow Wolf had killed; pieces with porcupine quill work; stone tomahawks; and old buffalo-hide Indian suitcases.

"If he liked you, you'd know right away, and if he didn't, well, you'd know *that* right away too. He'd say about some smart alec, 'I should've put an arrow in him,' " remembered a friend.[25] Lone Wolf for all his protestations proved himself a friend to the Mormons by donating one of the biggest paintings he had ever done (5x8 feet), depicting Jacob Hamblin in "A Mission Among the Indians" to the Eagar ward, which was hung in their chapel.

Lone Wolf called them "dudies," and about the only place in Greer, then, for an outsider to light was at Mollie and John Butlers'. Mollie Crosby had married a son of Jacob Noah Butler, John T., in 1908; become postmistress the same year; operated a small store out of the south end of her home; and added three children to the family, Willis, born 1910; Vince, 1913; and a niece, Cora Gibbons; and perhaps inadvertently, found her home north of her parents' old place gradually becoming the magnet for both relative and stranger—neither of whom she turned away.

The next tourist to come (in 1919) drove a Twin 6 Packard touring car. Greer was about the first place in Arizona the J. E. Thompson family stopped on their way West from New York where Thompson had earned enough in the investment banking business to retire at forty-two. His brother was William Boyce Thompson of copper fame. The J. E. Thompson family settled in Phoenix, but often stayed with John and Mollie Butler, and finally decided in the early twenties to have Butler build them a "place" on the hilltop coming into Greer. "The place" was the grandest thing around the country recalled a resident of Greer—It could sleep twenty-two people and had a main log lodge which had two fireplaces, five bedrooms upstairs, a living-dining room-kitchen on the main floor, and a bedroom suite on a lower level.

Mrs. Thompson had a mild case of TB and because her husband wanted her to rest in Greer, insisted all the furniture be rustic—with no varnish. She went down and ordered a piano someplace and when it arrived, it gleamed! In order to "blemish" it properly and therefor "take the work out of it," the village people were invited up and told to bring their branding irons. The spread also included guest cottages for Judge Charles

Ayer, New York, general counsel and later president of Newmont Mining Company, and another for William H. Remick of the New York Stock Exchange.

Mollie Butler's niece, Cora, remembered a conversation between John Butler and Thompson:

> Said John Butler, 'Well Ed, [Thompson] I'm quitting.'
>
> 'What's the matter, Johnnie?'
>
> 'You promised me a job all the time and there's a few hours in the night I don't have anything to do.'[26]

Thompson kept things going around the village with building, plumbing jobs, bringing parties in for hunting and fishing expeditions up on the mountain, where he had a permanent lean-to built on the west fork of the Little Colorado. The Thompsons' wealth and ways became almost legendary to people unaccustomed to such things. They were referred to locally always as "Wall Street millionaires." One remembered a horse trained for the circus that knelt for Mrs. Thompson to get on; another that they always had at least two servants working for them; another that their horses were driven (not motored) back and forth to Phoenix each season; another remembered the special Christmases Thompson would send gifts and decorations to the village children; and another as a child was fascinated by the sight of the couple coming down the footpath of "their hill" with long walking sticks.

But the Thompsons didn't see themselves exactly that way—He was a developer at heart, very involved getting things "fixed up" around the village. As the first around to have indoor plumbing, he encouraged the development of a big spring southwest of the village to serve all the residences in the main town area (as it yet does). The Butlers soon built their first bathroom at the north end of the front porch and water was gradually piped into various homes which had always been "supplied" by buckets of water taken from the stream or a nearby spring.[27]

Meanwhile other changes were occurring on a less grand scale. In 1916 the Mormon families of Greer were organized as a dependent branch of the Eagar ward under the leadership of Hyrum D. Nelson who had brought about 80-95 people out of Mexico because of the revolution there. The people settled between Benny and Rosey Creeks in what were described as shacks with board roofs that leaked like strainers. Nelson operated a sawmill on the site for a time.

World War I had claimed the time of a few local men; and prohibition, introduced in Arizona in 1915, encouraged bootleggers and moonshiners. The stills on mountain streams made the reputation of several local sheriffs who would stop at nothing to track down the sources of supply. A dance hall seven miles northwest of Greer, The Pahaska Lodge, was remembered as a bootlegging outfit—"a real bad place"—but the dancing was good.

"More people came in after World War I—Things really changed in Greer. Model T cars came in—They didn't use as many wagons and horses. Many people left Greer, but then lots moved in," remembered Mae Wiltbank.[28]

If life seemed rigorous to the pioneer, "life behind the wheel" seemed equally adventuresome to the early motorists who came into the high country. The more safe and sane place to go, especially for Phoenicians, was Iron Springs—a tourist colony near Prescott which could be reached by a decent road, or even better, by rail.

Some had made the trip up by wagon from the desert over the sixty-mile Roosevelt Road (later, "Apache Trail")—hacked out of the canyon between Mesa and Roosevelt to carry supplies to the Roosevelt Dam project—the "trail" looking more like a dry, boulder-strewn stream bed than anything else. The wagon trip up to the high country took weeks; but whether by wagon or auto, the route from both Phoenix and Tucson areas was the same (unless one chose the circle through Wickenburg, Prescott, Flagstaff, etc.). Once reaching Globe, travelers went through San Carlos Reservation—from Globe to Rice was twenty-two miles; Rice to Casadora Springs on Sycamore Creek, fifteen miles; Casadora Springs to Government Sawmill, seven miles; twenty-one miles to the Black and White (over which was a covered bridge, the only one in Arizona) Rivers, then on to Fort Apache and White River Indian Agency.

It was twenty-one miles from White River Agency to Cooley's Ranch (near present Indian Pine) where (about 1917) an early travel book said

> ... One finds the old pioneer scout, [Cooley] full of stories of the Apache raid days, and who, with his hospitable family, takes good care of guests and travelers, whether they are passing by and stop but for a meal, or come for a month.[29]

From there one could venture forth, refreshed, off the beaten path to Sheep's Crossing, ford streams and go further—or to Greer. Aunt Mollie remembered one fellow who came in and said it had taken him three years to get to Greer from McNary! Most made it in two and one-half days from Phoenix or Tucson.

It wasn't considered safe to take children on those kinds of trips, remembered the daughter of an early Greer visitor. But another early tourist, Milt Coggins Sr., remembered making the trip up from Phoenix and not even their touring car with bronze radiator was immune to the eighteen tire failures they had on one camping expedition. The job of removing the high-pressure tire and tube, easily punctured; patching it;

The Cooley Ranch

pumping it back up by hand; and "reattaching" was tedious. Low-powered, open cars, coupled by ruts, potholes, mud, sand, one-way roads with hairpin curves around cliffs, and large trees that seemingly grew out of the middle of the road were enough to convince travelers they were either mad or should never venture forth without a good "push team" along.[30]

Most of the first tourists camped—anywhere that looked good and wherever they could drive. A few went to Sheep's Crossing, including the Frank H. Carlock and (Dr.) William Holt (Old Dominion Mine doctor) families of Globe. They went by way of Greer, and camped up on the mountain the summer of 1921 for a month or so. After the families asked someone for instructions to get somewhere, the cook they had brought along, "Kentuc," retorted succinctly:

> De sitiation ain't, as I sees it, how far 'dis from here—But de question is weder *anybody* ever got 'der from here.[31]

63

RICE to FORT APACHE
and COOLEYS' 84.1 mi.

Rough Road - Long
Heavy Grades

Mileage reads Rice
and Springerville.

Key

☐ = When traveling
northerly or westerly
mileage from starting
pt. is in the square;
Southerly, easterly, in
Circle.

■ = house - with
"R" ranch; "P.O"- post-
office

H.C. = high centers

= sand

= location of
gate passed
through

= bridge

= telegraph, telephone
or power
line

To Snowflake
+ Holbrook

Cooleys
Ranch

49.1 [84.1]

Heavy
Grades

Rocks

48.7 [78.5]

22%

H.S.

Rocky

Rocky

H.S.

Rocky

Indian

☐ Huts

Gutters

☐ House

61.6 [65.6]

White River
P.O.

72.7 [54.5]

Rocky
H.C.

Indian
Agency

X

Rocks H.C.

66.7 [60.5]

Fort
Apache

15.7 [1.5]

Gutters - Washes

22%

Rocky

White River

79.1 [48.1]

Rocky

Fine Road
Wonderful Scenery
Rocky

Steep

Black = River
Tuttles Ranch

85.2 [36.8]

Summit

91.3 [35.9]

Fine
views

6 mile grade
Rocky + Steep.

Rocky

Pine Forests

Rough

90.4 [36.8]

Saw Mill

100.2 [27.]

102.3 [24.9]

105.1 [22.1] Divide

Grand views of
mountains + valleys

4 mi grade
6 to 22%

Rocky
grades

Cassador
Springs

Stony
Mesa

☐ Indian
Huts

125.7 [1.5]

To Globe

Indian School

Rice

Ford

127.2 [000]

To San Carlos

N

Mileage
in ☐

West

East

in ◯

Taken from:
Ariz. Good Roads Assoc.
Illustrated Road Map
Tour Book
Copyrighted: 1913 - Arizona
Good Roads Assoc., Prescott

64

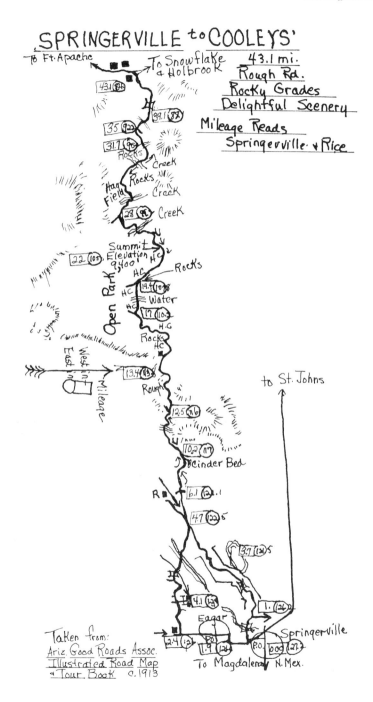

SPRINGERVILLE to COOLEYS'

To Ft. Apache   To Snowflake   43.1 mi.
& Holbrook   Rough Rd.
Rocky Grades
Delightful Scenery

Mileage Reads
Springerville & Rice

43.1 (84)
39.1 (87)
35 (92)
31.7 (96)
Rocks
Creek
Rocks   Creek
Hay Field   Creek
28 (99)   Creek

22 (105)   Summit
Elevation
9,400'
HC
HC   Rocks
HC   19.4 (107)
HC   Water
17 (110)
H.G
Rocks
HC

East   West in   13.4 (113)
Mileage   Rough

125 (116)

10.2 (117)
cinder Bed

R   6.1 (121).1

4.7 (122) 5

3.7 (124) 5

to St. Johns

T   4.1 (123)   1 (126)

2.4 (12)   P.O.   P.O.
1.9 (124)   .009 (27)
Eagar   Springerville

To Magdalena N. Mex.

Taken from:
Ariz. Good Roads Assoc.
Illustrated Road Map
& Tour Book   c. 1913

65

Rains came and the party couldn't get out. The men started worrying about their jobs and getting the children home for school. Finally the families were extricated from the summer's mud by John Butler coming up from Greer by wagon and pulling them out with a team. The family said twenty years later the tracks from that trip could still be seen on the cienega.

The first campers were looked at in amazement by the natives. They'd never seen anything like the outfitting done by the people—cars packed with gear on running boards, in trunks, strapped anywhere it would stay on. They brought wall tents, dutch ovens; some shipped up to a thousand pounds of provisions by parcel post; and found their various ingenious ways to creature comfort. The rainy season began anytime one decided to go camping, so one woman rigged a kind of hammock for the inside of the car to escape the rain—which, after collapsing on the horn, woke everyone in the village. Many used the mail service that went from Greer into Round Valley three times a week to bring back groceries. Eggs, butter, raw milk, vegetables, homemade breads and rolls were sold to tourists by some local women. Some baked as many as fourteen loaves of bread a day in the ovens of their wood cook stoves.

Through the years campers increased until some areas became almost like tent cities—at the end of the west fork road, at the Greer lakes, and beside almost any accessible (or inaccessible) stream or lake. People brought up old trailers and parked them; built on lean-tos out of old crates; pitched tents, adding to them from year to year, "personalizing" their claim, doing their own bit of homesteading. Their set-ups were considered just as inviolate, until they were vacated for good—That might be a matter of years.

Most of the first tourists came to fish, and what didn't exist at the tip of their pole, wasn't very memorable. But the fishing was enough. Golden yellow natives up to eleven inches were everywhere and the limit in the mid-1920s was twenty-five. Once, after he and his brothers complained of poor fishing and wanted to move camp, Milt Coggins Sr. recalled his father suggested putting down his Ingersol watch and when his dad said, "Go," all three went out to try to get a fish and whoever got back to camp first, won. They were all back in three minutes, so fishing wasn't considered to be very bad, and they didn't move on.

Telescopic rods, dry flies, and single action reels were brought into the village that had long known the knack of bending a pin for a hook, twisting thread for line, using a willow pole, and pieces of cork and whittled wood as bobs for lake fishing.

Camp at Squirrel Spring

Fishing season began the first of June and ended in September until the time of World War II. Stocking began in the twenties as there was a State Fish Hatchery at Squirrel Spring (near Benny Creek) at that time. Later there were four rearing ponds at Government Springs where one man remembered seeing hundreds of empty gallon Redheart dog food cans around, used to feed the fish. At that time fingerlings were being stocked, as rearing fish to a respectable size hadn't been perfected. Eventually fish were trucked, then taken by pack horse into even the most remote areas.

Many people came to hunt deer, elk, antelope, bear, and turkey. (The Merriam elk became extinct in the 1890s; the grizzly bear in the 1930s.) Deer, wild turkey, and bear season lasted from October 16 to November 15 in 1929. The Greer Refuge, or White Mountain Game Protective Association, was formed (lasting into the 1940s) to preserve some of the local game. Turkey were so plentiful in the area, Ed Dentzer Jr. could remember seeing rows of them nesting in trees near Amberion Point. "Gobblers would come swooping off the hillside, off the point, land on the roof of the cabin—The whole place would shake," he reported.[32]

Some tourists began to buy land (for $25-$100 per acre) and have cabins built. The whole village would often help on the job, with John Butler usually in charge. Sites were leveled to size by team; the logs, some as long as forty feet, cut by ax and crosscut saw, drug in by team; bark

67

peeled; laid up on rock foundations using ropes, rollers, even teams to get the top logs rolled up. Local shingles were often used for some siding and roofs. In addition to strips of lumber nailed between logs, needed chinking might be anything from mud mixed with hay, hemp, pieces of cork bark fir, or even newspaper. Cabins of the settlers were often dovetailed logs, fitting without nails or dowels. Later construction was more often a squared notch or in some, logs nailed into a vertical corner post. Fireplaces were *de rigueur* for desert dwellers but many natives' homes kept warmer with stoves. Aspen was used mainly for decorative banisters on indoor stairs and balconies, along porches, and for cross beams spanning the ceilings.

Water dictated locations (since wells, at best, went little deeper than a shovel's length). Springs were tapped with pipes sometimes extending distances of six thousand feet. The Redington cabin at Amberion Point used a hydraulic ram set in the stream that pumped water from the west fork up one hundred feet to a fifty gallon gas drum above the cabin. The system operated until 1969 with not more than thirty-five cents in repairs—Only thing that would stop it would be a curious fisherman picking up the pipe. That shut off the system every time, commented a subsequent owner.[33]

City folk learned the rigors of wild animals inside and out. Even "tame ones"—Many were rattled by the proprietary bellow of a village milk cow as she announced her claim to all grazing rights beyond their back door. They dug garbage pits, chopped wood, lit kerosene lamps and pumped up gas ones whose mantles exploded into flame when first lit. They used privys outside and thunder mugs inside; kept their food in metal drums and screened burlap-covered coolers attached to the outside of the cabin. (Local people had long before found rock-lined dugouts or cellars ideal for winter vegetable storage, and in summer, submerged things in a cold spring nearby.) "Transplanted" children were sometimes kept safe from rodents in screen-covered kiddie coops inside.

Among those building cabins then, and the approximate dates, were: the Fred Winns from Tucson, 1922;[34] the Clay Parkers from Phoenix, 1925; the Coffin-Cornish-Stark-Clark place, 1925; the Bill Studors of Tempe, 1925; the C.H. Redingtons from Stockton, Calif., 1929; G.H. Coffins from Phoenix, 1929; Henry Mayhews of Tucson, 1930; "the Crow's Nest" occupied by E. G. Crow, truant officer at Phoenix Union High School, 1930. On the east fork, the government had opened areas for summer homes and two spinster school teachers, Toni McCarigan and Ruth Newcomb built the first cabin in about 1929. (Miss Newcomb

"The Crow's Nest"

taught in Greer several years too.) Next to build there were the Bob Hughes of Miami and in 1932, the Harmon Keyes. The Presbyterian summer camp, Montlure, was also built at the end of that road and opened for sessions the summer of 1932.

In 1923 Cliff Wentz, who had been given six months to live because of TB, drove into Greer in a Model T Ford with his father, William J. Settling there year round, they built a house on the site of the old E.W. Wiltbank sawmill. Both lived to be old men. Cliff, obscured behind thick glasses, was essentially blind—but he had a feel for machines. Since everything in the village was run by gas motors, he was busy. He gardened, baked bread, was an avid fisherman, and a pretty fair carpenter. Even though he had never clearly seen any of it, he had an intuitive feel for the country, could describe exactly where each fork of the road led, and often helped guide on pack trips.[35]

"My father's idea of camping or traveling at all, for that matter, was to find the nearest hotel," said Fritzie Ryley of her father, Judge Fred Struckmeyer of Phoenix.[36] He quickly found Butlers', as did many others.

Mollie Butler said of the lodge which "officially" started in 1908, "At first it was a free lodge where anyone could come and stay when hunting, fishing, or vacationing. There were beds all over the place. One person would get wood, another water, another would do other chores."[37] Mollie's daughter, Hannah, who had worked in the informally-run boarding house for some time, finally got up enough nerve to start charging guests—at first only twenty-five cents per meal.

Gradually rooms and buildings were added, somehow becoming attached to each other—the square house, the long house, the log lodge later known as "the Bluebird" with all the names carved on the inside of the door. Later a carbide system, buried in front with pipes leading to outlets in all the rooms, provided "gaslight." Around the hill, south of the lodge, the Butlers built six rental cabins with running water piped to a faucet behind the places—immortalized as "Pee-can Row" by an early renter.

Relatives, young and old; itinerate teenagers of one variety or another were gathered in to cook for and clean the lodge, which eventually served seventy to one hundred meals a day and could sleep twenty to thirty. Most of the food, served family style, was "from scratch"—perpetuating the old ways that once were necessities, but to tourists were luxuries: homemade butter, jams, breads, desserts, cheeses, fresh eggs and homegrown chickens, and vegetables from the garden.

The famous and the not-so-famous were loaded up and taken on outings, picnics, and hunting trips by John Butler. His stories and antics brightened the day of many children and oldsters and he was fondly remembered:

> I found John Butler one of the real characters of Greer. He was a very interesting man—very active, had been all his life. I'm not sure, like a lot of other characters, whether you could believe everything John told you, but he could tell you a lot of interesting things and knew a great deal about hunting and fishing and that sort of thing.[38]

One of the highlights of the summer for tourist and native alike were the roundups of the Greer allotment, a USFS grazing permit shared by different cattle owners in the vicinity. As the cattle were rounded up, people would gather at the Slade Ranch (owned by the Butlers) to watch as the cowboys identified every cow and calf, and called the brand as each was brought in for branding, denutting, de-horning, marking of ears, and vaccinations. Vince Butler was remembered as the expert at calling the right brand of each calf. The three-day event ended with a bounteous pot-luck, somehow brought together and served out of a tiny ranch house kitchen equipped with one wood stove, often to hundreds.

The Butler herd had grown from the one milk cow given Mollie by her father as a bride, to a herd of 250 cattle. In addition were the horses, both working and those used as rental for the lodge guests.

Old Slade Cabin

(Early Brands of the Area)

MY	John T & Molly Butler
X	Willis Butler
+L	Vince Butler
A	Geo. Crosby
NKY	Cleve Wiltbank
	Mit Wiltbank
HD	Henry Day
r	Marion Lantz
{6-6	Harry Udolf }
20	Fred Dark Family
Z	Joe Pierce
YP	Howard Hale
A SL	Milo Wiltbank
	Sam Love
	Sarah Ann Butler
HDF	Fred Hoffman
U-C	Frank Brinkley Later Al Voight

Vince Butler
May 28 1979

71

Mollie Butler remained a mixture of progressiveness, graciousness, and pragmatism. She kept well-polished floors that showed up a fake the minute he or she crossed the threshold. She loved a good poker game after dinner; and raised up many a child, both summer and winter, returning them home at least a couple of inches greater in stature from her love and care. More than one can remember her hollering into an extension of the Forest Service line in the dining room—She could be heard at the end of the road, but not at the end of the line. William Thompson (son of J.E.) called her from Los Angeles to check on his two boys staying at the lodge. He yelled, she yelled; he couldn't hear her, she could hear him. Finally through the static broke her exasperated voice: "What are you worrying about those two boys for? They're twice as smart as you ever were!"[39]

The woman whose guest list included Zane Grey, Stuart Edward White, the Herbert Hoovers, Governors George W.P. Hunt and John Phillips, and a young lady remembered, a man from Tucson who would always offer kids a dollar if they could stand on their heads for a minute, still rose before dawn to churn butter; making her own soap and bedding—quilts, sheets, and cases which she bleached on the snow; and slept nearly her whole life on a corn-husk mattress. Her niece, Cora Sharp, recalled her "mama"—

> She was—She made everybody do things, you know? She was kindhearted, but she expected everything to be done. Maybe she was hardhearted, I don't know. I remember when Papa [John Butler] died, why she leaned over the casket and said, 'I'll live to bury you all.' I never saw her cry—probably did—went to her bedroom and cried. But she was just that kind of a person. She was kind of the leader of her whole family, far's that's concerned, of the whole other family. She liked people. In the winter, if she didn't have someone to cook for, she'd cook great big things and give to the neighbors.[40]

"Business" was beginning to diversify in Greer. Though every available piece of land was cultivated—potatoes, beautiful grain fields, garden crops, and stock grazed—one eye was kept on the evolving tourist trade and how to serve it. Beginning in 1912, Greer bought a section in *Arizona State Business Directory*, listing local businesses for one-year periods. Among them were (though some were listed who lived elsewhere but "were available"):

1918-19

Butler, M., postmaster
Butler & Wiltbank, bakery
Greer, S., lumber

1924-25

Butler, John T., boarding
   house, carpenter
Butler, Mollie, postmaster

Hall & Windsor, live Stock	Butler & Wiltbank, carpenters
Jefcoat, Robert, shoemaker	Day, Henry, ice
Nelson, Jas., blacksmith	Crosby, George H., lawyer
Robins, Margaret, prin. sch.	Haynes, George L., barber
Robinson, M.G., physician	Hamblin, Josephine, prin. sch.
Wiltbank, Dora, dressmaker	Wiltbank W.E. & Co., live
Wiltbank, E.W., lumber	Stock[41]

In those years, as far as the job of postmaster was concerned, he or she was paid the amount of the stamp cancellation—So one of Mollie's children remembered she didn't mind their sending off for tubes of toothpaste, and other paraphernalia from catalogues. The job was passed on to Atella Haws in 1924-26, while she was living in Greer with her husband Carl. After that it went to John C. Wiltbank, who operated it out of one end (or another) of his home from 1926 to 1958.

During the mid-twenties, Marion Lund not only had the mail contract, but was listed in the business directory as freighting and running a stage line. Part of his "line" was his sister-in-law, Erma Macdonald (later "Burk"), who lived with them and three times a week drove a light spring wagon with a team in for the mail. Only the last two years of Lund's eight-year contract did he use a Ford pickup. When the post office was at the Wiltbanks the mail was "delivered." A fellow later remembered,

> [There was] some old gal who had a two-door coupe. She was the lady that drove the mail in from Springerville. She used to wear gloves—By God, the car would drive up, this old lady would get out with her gloves and little bag and she'd carry it very officiously, carry those things in there, and Mrs. Wiltbank would sort the mail.[42]

George E. Crosby, married to Florence Greer in 1922, (Her grandfather, Thomas L. Greer, was Americus Vespucious' brother.) decided to open a store south of the lodge in 1927. Logs for the 16x16-foot room cost a total of $1.98. At first gas was pumped from barrels, later from a visible pump. The first "family store" had been over at the Crosby homestead on a knoll by the fork of the Black. For a time his aunt, Cora Ida Gibbons, and her husband had a store on the side of the hill, south of the village; then Mollie, his mother, ran one out of the Butler home where she carried a few canned goods; staple items; sold hunting and fishing licenses; and dried fruit—pears, peaches, raisins, packed in cellophane in twenty-five pound boxes.

The Crosbys later built another store south of the log structure—larger, with living quarters in the back and above the store. Groceries and gas were hauled from Holbrook by truck. Two things

Crosby carried that made his store unique in the area—vegetables pulled right from the garden beside the store and stuffed in one's sack (together with free dirt); and the ice he cut from the Greer lakes during the winter, stored in sawdust in a tunnel near the lakes, then in the summer hauled to an ice house near the store. No other lakes produced ice thick enough to use, and George Crosby recalled supplying ice to Johnny LeSueur who ran the Saffell Hotel in Springerville. Edward G. Dentzer Sr., retired and living in Greer year round at the time, helped Crosby with the ice on occasion, but tired of the exhausting work—cutting the ice into two-foot thick blocks, hauling the 200 pound blocks up on to the surface of the lakes, then using horses to drag them to the tunnel. Dentzer decided to mount a gas-driven crosscut-type saw on a sled which, reported his son, made the whole thing much easier.[43]

Besides working the store and service station, as their family grew to seven children, the Crosbys did what everybody else did—a lot. They farmed; ran cattle, rented horses, conducted pack trips; had a few rental units; sold hand-separated milk from their own cows; gathered eggs, slopped and butchered pigs and hogs; hayed cows and horses; gardened; raised crops; washed in tubs outside, and tried to get everyone clean for the Saturday night dance and Sunday school in one tub inside. For both "jobs" it meant, in most households, heating water in kettles over a wood fire and pouring it in the tubs.

The depression hit toward the end of 1929. One family left Greer, selling their 160 acre ranch for $500 and others sold back land to the government for one dollar an acre (i.e., along the east fork). By the thirties the copper markets began to disappear and the price of copper, farm products, and livestock plummeted. For some, living in Arizona mining towns where the mines were shutting down, came their first vacation. In 1930 the Dentzer family in Miami loaded up and took a three month trip through the state—winding up the Coronado Trail and finding Greer in the course of their travels. Remembered Art Leeds of his first visit to the valley in 1934:

> The village looked like a frontier. They were building new cabins.... I was much impressed by the village because at that time, during the depression, they seemed to be going along more smoothly than they were in the larger towns

and cities like Phoenix; and everybody seemed to be happy and doing something. They wasn't making much money, but they seemed to be enjoying what they were doing, and seemed to be a happy people.[44]

One of the projects of Franklin Roosevelt's New Deal government to pull the country out of its crisis was the Civilian Conservation Corps and Greer had some 300 people at a CCC camp near Benny Creek in the late thirties. Composed of eighteen to twenty-five year olds, the nationwide conservation program built 1,500 camps, mainly in forested areas. Living under army discipline, the boys received $30 per month plus food, clothing, medical attention, and education. In Arizona, 9,000 corpsmen lived and worked in over forty camps.[45]

The young men from the Benny Creek camp realigned the west fork road, blasted out stumps of big trees, and put in metal cattle guards and gates; put little log spillway dams on creeks clear up to the reservation; built a new ranger station in 1939; cleared trails and improved picnic areas. Up on the mountain, an area that had once been just a slough was dammed up in 1934 by the CCC and Big Lake was created. In some notes John Butler made, he remarked that a good road was built into Greer by the Forest Service in 1936.[46]

But nothing dimmed the doings at the school house—the hub of the community. By the thirties the school was frame with a bell on top which later fell off and was hung from a tower northeast of the school. The building was still used for Sunday school. (By 1930 church records show about nine Mormon families lived in Greer and John Butler was presiding elder.)[47] And on a rotating basis, some child was paid seven dollars a month to be janitor of the school house.

Native and tourist alike gathered for the community bonfires and dances. A camper remembered a sheepherder who walked from Big Lake for the Saturday night affairs, and liked to dance with Mollie Butler. One visiting young lady in knickers felt herself no match (for the cowboys' attention) to the pretty local girls who changed into summery dresses in the evening for the dance after having done piles of dishes and cleaned all day. After more thought, she concluded that the local girls were probably better dancers too.[48] One "regular" remarked that in the course of the evening some usually ended up climbing the bell tower.

Ed Dentzer Jr. could always tell if there was going to be a dance by looking from his house at Amberion Point, north across the meadow to the Lunds', to see if they had a fire in back. If they did, it meant they

Greer School House

Montlure — 1931

were heating water to take baths and the dance was "on." He also remembered some unannounced affairs at the boarded-up Thompsons' Lodge that had a player piano in it:

> The Montlure kids would go to bed at the regular time. Pretty soon they'd all get up, crawl out the upstairs windows, down on the roofs of the lower rooms, down the post, then hike down to the Thompson place and have a dance almost every Saturday night.[49]

It still took eight to keep the school in session, which meant some years they were only in the market for teachers with children. Afton Wiltbank's son Jack remembered being enrolled at three years of age because things were tight that year. But the most fun came during lunch and recess. During the spring and fall, some would build willow teepees and heat their lunch in them. Roads traversed the hill behind the school for the travels of toy cars—Swings were located on just the right tree to send a child shooting out over a cliff. In the winter there was sledding and skiing—off the hill, down and around the trees, past the school house, down past the Lunds', and through Grandma (Sarah) Butler's gate across the road (which had been opened just in case). That was the course for the ski race every recess—And they could just about make it in the twenty minutes allotted. (The skis just had a strap for the foot to slip into.) For sledding, they'd use the same course with a little water poured over to make it slicker.[50]

Two other couples came in whose projects kept Greer busy and fascinated. One was the home built in the late thirties by James and Cornelia Baird on the hill, southwest of the store. The Bairds, originally from New York, lived in Tucson. He had been construction engineer for the Lincoln Memorial; New York's beloved Flatiron building (the country's first steel skyscraper); the Folger Shakespeare Memorial Library, Washington, D.C.; and on one of the last jobs before his death (1953), Baird constructed a swimming pool in the White House for FDR. Before he sold his hilltop place, he sat in the living room there and remarked to the new buyers (Ward and Mary Gillespie), "I've built some beautiful buildings, but this is the most beautiful of all."[51]

Mrs. Baird had a slight figure and a bit of the fey about her. She would carry jumping beans and pockets full of pecan ice box cookies for the village kids. Walking down the road, playing her harmonica, she was the understated, dignified pied piper of the town—One could almost imagine a gathering of faithful fans stringing out behind her, ready to follow her lead.

East of River Reservoir on 245 acres of patented and 800 acres of leased land, the Bob Evans family was planning a dude ranch as a summer extension of the Evans' Jokake Inn in Phoenix, on the site of the old Burk Ranch. The idea was people would come from the East by rail to Holbrook where they would be met. Fred Burk cut most of the logs for the place which was built in 1938-39. All of log, it had five cabins, each having two bedrooms with fireplaces; and a main lodge with several bedrooms, kitchen, dining, living and game rooms, and office. The logs were squared off on three sides with rounded side out, grooved along their length and stacked up with a 1"x1" key that fit into the grooves, holding the logs together.

"Adobe Bob" (the name applied to the builder of adobe homes for tourists in Phoenix) embarked on his Greer project with gusto, first forging a road past the ranger station to his resort. Before, the E.R. DeWitts, John Eagars, Duane Hamblins, David Bigelows, Fred Burks, and Henry Days had slithered over the River Reservoir dam to get to their property. Some of the locals thought a bathroom and fireplace for every bedroom was sort of crazy. When the building was complete, Evans told his daughter to run down to the "interior decorating department" of Beckers for furnishings! Jokake had its own generating plant, forced-air heating, ice plant, and brought its own string of horses up from Phoenix for the summer season.

When the Evans were ready to have a house warming, they called up to ask the Springerville telephone operator how to get the word around. With fifteen on the party line on the USFS extension, they had a start—Then the operator suggested putting up signs in Springerville, Eagar, and Greer. Everybody found out about it and the whole countryside turned out.

Running a lodge in the mountains was interesting, foreign, and sometimes hard for the Valley of the Sun family. Evans' daughter and son remembered that they had to sterilize and separate their own milk, taking up two cows from the Mission Dairy in Phoenix that had to be inspected. There was some worry about "their cows" mixing with the uninspected local cows that grazed side by side. And the laundry was a problem: They had to take the dirty things back to Phoenix, usually by Mariano (an employee from Scottsdale). One time driving Highway 60, Mariano ran off the road, but jumped out of his truck before it went over the bank. He was saved, but the truck was totalled, and the sheets, towels, and pillow cases were strewn all over the highway.[52]

The pre-World War II era closed with the death (in 1940) of two men whose personal expansiveness made them natural and effective promoters

of the area. In Springerville, Gustav Becker, pioneer of modern state highways, Apache County highway engineer, died at eighty-three—never to see the final completion of his favorite project, U.S. 60 through Salt River Canyon. At his death, fifty-six miles remained unpaved, though the bridge across the Salt had been completed (in 1934) and the road was graveled.[53]

And in Greer, John T. Butler was dead at fifty-four. Said his son, Vince:

> I remember him as one of the finest men that I ever knew—He loved people, he loved life. He was a carpenter, a jack-of-all-trades. Primarily [he] did most of the building in Greer when the tourists and recreationalists started coming in. He built most of their houses; did their plumbing; cut the logs; furnished the horses and teams and the other men to do the work. At his funeral one of the Superior Court judges . . . said he [John Butler] and my mother were probably the best ambassadors to Apache County we'd ever had.[54]

V

No More Apron Strings

Death's erratic but unbeatable system picked its time and number, and war broke out across the oceans—Young men rushed off breathlessly to meet its challenge; while too-young boys stayed home, moved up a notch or two, filled boots yet a little generous, and swaggered out to do a man's work in the village where everyday chores hadn't changed one whit, war or no war; and the "no-nonsense sameness" of the place, the people, and their doings seemed sane and durable. "Outside" the foundations of old-world societies were being shot out from under them as man's voracious appetite for territorial power was choking on gun powder.

If one had the gas stamps there was still homemade butter served in Greer; anyone could have anything he or she wanted for breakfast at Butlers'—as long as it was bacon and eggs and flapjacks; some kids were going to school on the "potato plan" (home-grown potatoes in exchange for a school lunch); down in the meadow of an evening there were community bonfires where they were still playing "Kick the Can" and "Drop the Handkerchief"; and someone, somewhere on a bet might just "take you up on that" and repeat the alphabet backwards.

The girls and women were most generally wrapped up in washing, ironing, cooking, housekeeping; and the men and boys were outside where there were wide open spaces and fresh, cool, thin, air to breathe in so deep it ached—and a big enough piece of the Old West alive in every male heart to assure that it wouldn't die for a while.

The initiation rites into manhood could be gone through locally, even if one was a little underage—for there were big 2½ ton Chevy stake trucks, wild horses, and pretty girls to be chased, conquered, and tamed—And playing cowboy in Greer was an irresistible attraction for many a kid-at-heart.

For a "cowboy," most chores —plowing, weeding, the whole farm-yard scene was to be avoided if at all possible (It usually wasn't!); and the thing was, to get out of there as soon as possible (when no one was look-ing), in a truck, on a horse, and high-tail it up on the mountain! There were other things that came under the guise of "work," but quali-fied under "cowboy"—shooting a piece of livestock for butchering; shooting prairie dogs so horses wouldn't get caught in their burrows and break a leg; picking off rats from a cabin wall with a .22 caliber; chasing a bunch of turkey on foot until a few fell in their tracks, ex-hausted, and resigned to becoming the main dish for dinner; helping out with pack trips; packing fish into the back country for stocking by horse or jeep; chasing bulls to keep them out of people's hair (really, just for the fun of it); scaring some city kid out of his mind and up a tree with a bear-scenario, carefully enacted; or breaking bronco horses—which wasn't taken up by just anyone.

Roy Hall was pretty well known for that activity. One evening when

A Cowboy

Zane Grey and his brother were guests at Butlers' Lodge, John Butler had brought the party up to where Hall was working horses.

> John ask [sic] me to give them a little exhibition riding, which I did. Zane was quite impressed with the bucking horses, and maybe a little with the riding. Anyhow, he ask me to go with them out on the mountain on a hunting trip. He said he would pay me $10.00 a day, which was good money in those days. I was to take along some of the broncos so when things got too dull, there would be some bronco riding. Next morning we left Greer. I was to be horse wrangler as well as entertainer.[1]

Everyone remembered the "Cowboy Reunions" held in Round Valley on the Fourth of July. People knew the contestants—They were mostly local amateurs riding bareback for one dollar a time. Cora Sharp remembered the family being loaded into the wagon, hitching up "Dan" and "Cap," and going to Springerville for ice cream, the reunion, and the "chuck wagon race"—

> They were with wagon and a team—The cowboys got out and unhitched their horses, like they were putting them to feed; then unrolled their beds, got in their beds, slept a little while. Then they'd get up, roll up their bed, get in their wagon, put in their bedroll, then away they'd go with their team!—Chuck wagon race they called it.[2]

Later on, "imports" were passed off as qualified for competition. Bill Thompson (who became "Wallace" of the Phoenix TV show "Wallace and Ladmo"), grandson of J. E. Thompson, spent a whole summer in the mid-forties at Butlers' with his cousin Joe. They'd enter rodeos all over—St. Johns, Eagar—and get pitched every time. But nothing dimmed their enthusiasm and they didn't think their arena record bad for two fifteen-year-old boys from New York who had never been on a horse before.

Another summer cowboy during the 1940s was Paul Beer from Phoenix who went up and stayed with the Crosby family, got in on the same chores, and was treated just like any of the other Crosby kids. As far as the kids were concerned, the big treat was the weekly trip into Springerville in the Crosbys' 2½ ton Chevy truck on Wednesdays to meet the produce truck from Phoenix. This also meant going to the drug store and gorging on ice cream, looking at all the funny books, and buying some pulp song books.

On Saturday night were the Eagar dances which were considered (at that age), better than those of Greer because the latter were a little too traditional, didn't have quite the attendance and availability of girls that Eagar had. It might take the boys in Greer all week to hustle a ride if the stake truck wasn't available. There was one wealthy couple nearby with only one son—car, gas stamps—everything perfect. Only thing was, he could never have the car. It took time and ingenuity to get away from the Crosby house on a Saturday evening because of the one-bathtub situation. The first ones there got the hottest water because it was heated by the wood stove. Since the milkers always hit it last, that meant lukewarm water for them. So it was always "a fist fight" to see who got in there first. But once those things were cleared away, it was Springerville, the drug store, then the movie, and finally, the dance.

And there were endless plans and pranks—On VJ Day word got to Greer somehow and a couple of boys took a shotgun and rode over to Jokake, woke everyone up, and by accounts, "terrorized" that place. There were some surveyors staying in Butlers' square house that same night who got what was described as "knee-walkin' drunk" and were shooting off a .45 caliber pistol.

> One of the greatest things, greatest fun we ever had was Becker Mercantile had a great big billboard right up there at the crossroads where you turn off to go to Big Lake, where the sawmill is now—They had a big billboard that said 'Becker Mercantile'—One of the greatest fun we had, had a can of paint hid up there and we'd paint the lower part of that 'B' out so it'd read 'Pecker Mercantile Company.' And that'd drive old man Becker crazy.[3]

One "cowboy," grown into a fighter pilot, thought he'd say hello to the folks in Greer by buzzing the canyon in a National Guard P51. He hoped his "pass through" was fast enough that no one recognized him. (Although thirty-five years later, he still was waiting for someone to mention it.)

But the catalyst for all under-age cowboys was the roundup. That required getting on a horse, a rope, practicing one's knots and "nooses." Many kids vividly remembered the roundup camp with Vince Butler in charge of the crew, as the younger ones stationed themselves around the branding fire. While the cattle bawled and milled around, the cowboys would rope a calf, call the brand, and drag it in on a neck rope. The kids would scramble to meet it, flank it by getting one on the head, one on the tail, throwing it down and holding it there (often getting kicked in the process and rolling in the mud and dirt), while the older men branded.

No heart could resist the whirrr of the rope as it shot from the cowboys' hands like some snake seeking prey, and snapped around the neck of the calf. The thing was, to find a horse and get off in the woods with a rope, a decent loop, and try to "catch" a log, a kid brother or sister, or

another slow-moving object—even if it took a thousand tries and meant getting pitched on the fanny to do it!

Other vivid memories of the war years around Greer were of the plane crashes on or near Mount Baldy. Buelah and Ed Dentzer were awakened at three on a stormy morning by a plane circling so low over their Greer cabin it made the clouds appear red. The bomber crashed at the head of Bonita Creek, south of Baldy, the trees sliced off like a mowing machine had been through. Eleven or twelve were dead.

Then another Air Force plane went down east of Baldy on Burro Mountain. A hitchhiker riding in the tail of the plane survived the crash, fashioned splints and crutches out of the fuselage, but was eventually found dead from exposure under a tree a distance from the crash. The wreckage was found three or four months later, guns still loaded, and maps that were said to give the elevation of Baldy at 9,500 feet. Among the dead was the pilot, last name "Motley" from Texas. His mother, Helen, later came to Greer to see the site, stayed at Butlers', and eventually built a cabin.

A plane from Kirkland Air Force Base in New Mexico, searching for the Burro Mountain plane, crashed off the north side of Baldy. The four in the plane, two of whom were in "their Sunday shoes and just along for the ride," made their way through the snow to the peak. From there they sighted smoke coming from Whiteriver and headed down toward its source. Two died on the way down. The other two, their feet frozen, removed their shoes, then couldn't get them back on, and literally crawled into the Indian agency on their hands and knees. Later, one of the survivors returned to marry the girl who had nursed him during his stay at the reservation hospital.[4]

The Ed Dentzer Sr. family had moved up to Greer permanently after he retired in 1945 as general manager of Magma in Miami and became "fixtures" of sorts. They stayed at Amberion Point in the summer and in the winter moved to the north end of the valley on thirty-six acres they'd bought in 1935 from a J. T. Lewis of Globe. The property had a garage on it of dovetailed logs that dated before 1900, and a half-finished main house. Formerly a ship's carpenter, "J. T." was hired to finish up the house. He was precise, but would never use a level—said on a ship a level was no good—and did everything with a square. When the house was finished in 1937, Ed Dentzer Jr. remembered that other than Butlers', they were about the only ones with a toilet and all the pipes going into a septic tank. They, and eventually several other families, put in Kohler generating plants for lights.[5]

Thompsons' place was sometimes run as a lodge by the Crosbys who had acquired it; was sometimes closed up as was Montlure, which between 1941 and 1945 had become a "rat-infested" junk pile according to one disgruntled Presbyterian.[6]

As a forty-seven year old bride, Mary Ross Gillespie was brought to Greer on a vacation in 1941 by her husband Ward who was a dentist, and the couple bought Thompsons'. Calling Greer a "little bit of heaven," Mrs. Gillespie (the first M.D. to take an internship in anesthesiology at the state [Iowa] university), found it a wonderful interlude from a practice that began in 1923. A few years later they acquired the Baird home on the hill; sold Thompsons' to Milt and Althea Turner; and after retirement in 1958, spent six months—"until they were snowed out"—in Greer.[7]

Julian Herrod moved to Greer in 1947 without any credentials. He could neither read nor write nor remember when he was born nor how old he was; just that he was half Cherokee, and born in Ramona, Oklahoma. He was another local character who in the summer, worked for most everybody—Aunt Mollie, Vince Butler, George Crosby, Dean Coulter, Mrs. Ed Dentzer Sr.—and by his own account in the winter "didn't do nothing!" He was known to have a heart of gold, couldn't keep money because he'd loan his to anyone who needed it; ended up in the hospital from time to time, half-poisoned from the wrong food; and finally had to leave Greer in the 1970s after having a stroke.

Later at the Algiers Rest Home in Phoenix, he chewed a box of cigars a week that Coulter, a Phoenix Cadillac dealer, brought him; spasmodically dredging up garbled fragments of history—something about Adam's Diggins; Aunt Mollie and the Milk Ranch; riding George's Old Eagle over to Norton's to give grain to the wild turkey; about the dovetailed logs in the Dentzer garage; the steel telegraph poles Indians couldn't climb to cut the wires; about a Devil's—where there was a big hotel "they" just let tumble down; about places that changed hands so often it was pitiful; about having seen it thirty-eight degrees below—a sharp, agile mind that struggled to express itself through lips that stiffly refused to communicate: "I could tell you a lot of interesting stories if I could talk good."[8]

The Arthur E. Leeds family came with their two young children—about the last to try their hand at the "old ways" of settling in, earning a living. They bought five acres from the Fred Burks and started Leeds Northwoods in 1946 on the road that was the best bet from Greer to places like Sheep's Crossing, Big Lake, Cresent Lake, the Black and

White Rivers. At first there were only about twenty cars coming by their lonely outpost—a three-room house they had built themselves, with pens for chickens and pigs.

They later added a garage, selling gas from an old hand pump to the increasing number of sightseers and tourists who made their way up the steep road that joined the old wagon trail curving up the ridge from Badger Pond. (The wagon route was later incorporated into a USFS trail to Mount Baldy.) They piped water thousands of feet from a spring near Benny Creek to their home and rental units, cut ice off the lakes and stored it in an icehouse for summer trade. Lydia Leeds baked pies, bread, donuts, dressed hundreds of fryers to sell, and kept a ready coffee pot for those who weren't going anywhere, just wanted to visit around the fireplace. They wrestled with the problem of stretching a four month's income over twelve, and decided in 1959 to open a sawmill operation. The site and mill were later acquired by their son, Dan, who also had a pulpwood contract.[9]

"Later pioneers" also got in on a lot of conveniences of the "modern era" that came in rapid succession in the 1950-70s—Wells were sunk everywhere; and electricity, phones, TV reception, paved roads, and a library put in. The business community gradually geared itself toward skyrocketing land prices, an expanded season, and organized into citified civic clubs, chambers of commerce, etc.

Leland Entrekin, Phoenix minister with the velvet voice who had preached to thousands around the state on the radio program "Heart to Heart Hour" and had a church with the same name, came to Greer, rented, then built (1942) the first house in "Feudin' Acres"—a tag the Wiltbank-Butler land south of the village later acquired because people were always arguing about boundaries and water and whose was whose. Mrs. Entrekin had "feelings" about things. She used to take the family up for devotionals every evening on the site she felt would one day be theirs on which to build a cabin.

> Many times as I sat on the log looking down on the field that stretched to the road, I *felt* strongly, rather than 'saw' so much, the presence of a woman in a long dress. She seemed to be tending a garden. I couldn't see her face as it was hidden by a bonnet and her head bowed, but she seemed so sad and from time to time wiped tears from her eyes. After these times I would look up—startled I guess—and my children would ask me what the matter was.[10]

She later talked to Afton Wiltbank (who owned the property) about her "feelings" and Mrs. Wiltbank said her widowed mother, Dorthea Haws, had a potato patch in about that spot some forty years before, and Widow Haws was sometimes sad. That was about the only thing Mrs. Wiltbank could lay it to.

Donna Entrekin felt other indications about another site with a pear tree and remains of an old cellar on the "brow" overlooking the valley where the east and west forks joined. The Entrekins eventually bought this property from Rue Kimball, Mollie Butler's son-in-law, and in 1948 started the three-story log "Little Colorado Lodge" as a summer church facility for children and a place open for guests until June of the year. The lodge was sold to Ethel and Elmer Bellinger in 1960, who renamed it "Greer Lodge" and started a guest facility in earnest.

Other lodges and guest places started opening up: The Turners operated Hilltop; Paul and Ann Stephens had bought the old Lund place in 1942 and turned it into the White Mountain Lodge; Bob and Sylvia Reed of Springerville had bought Jokake; and Wayne and Irene Ziegler had a big family and housekeeping cabins on the old Howard Hale place. Ed and Buelah Dentzer cleared away some of the trees where the tom-turkeys had perched and Amberion had slept with his horses in a one-room hut, and built Amberion Point Lodge which opened in 1971.

The war was over and "the lights went on again, all over the world"—but for Greer they went on for the first time in 1950, when electricity was brought in and thirty-four customers in Greer were billed by Navopache Electric Co-Operative, Inc.[11] Sometime after, private phones came into Greer. Some felt the parent company in Holbrook was still using Alexander Graham Bell's original equipment in the whole area and the phone situation came under attack in a 1951 (n.d.) Phoenix *Arizona Republic* editorial:

> If the White Mountain people expect Phoenicians and others from south and central Arizona to come up to their cool, pine ... heights for summer vacations, they should at least make telephone service available more than twelve hours a day and two hours on Sunday .... Sometimes in small communities it is impossible to get the operator because she's out feeding her chickens.

Getting away from the switchboard had its advantages (to callers) as many could attest concerning the Springerville operator. From her headquarters, wherever that might have been (some swear it was a tower and she used binoculars), most of the comings and goings of the townspeople were known. When one called "Mrs. So-and-So" there was no need to surmise, after interminable rings, she wasn't in. The operator would

break in and might say, "Why, she's over to Becker's for a few minutes—just a second, that's her comin' out now—should be home in a few minutes. I'll tell her you was trying to get her."

Mollie Butler died in July, 1964 at eighty-seven. Said Ben Avery, the reporter who had written her obituary in the *Arizona Republic*:

> You couldn't write a story about Greer without talking to Aunt Mollie. I've always liked the folks in Greer. The flavor of Greer, what really made it interesting, stemmed as much from the people [like her] who lived there, the settlers, as anything else.[12]

She came to Arizona Territory in a covered wagon when she was six and flew by jet to Dallas at eighty-six. She had sorted through a lot of different ways of living that had passed by during her lifetime and seemed to know from the inside out what was right for her. She never realized the real value of the meals she served, the land she sold, but she had a rare collection of friends by the time she died.

Mollie Butler remained for most who knew her something of a leather-bound, first edition—tough, but not brittle with the years, absolutely straight forward—the kind one didn't expect to run across often.

The matriarch was gone, but her daughter Hannah and son-in-law Rue Kimball who had worked the lodge summer after summer decided to tear down the old Butler home that had become the gathering-eating-cooking part of the lodge, and build afresh. Hannah saw the foundations poured in the spring of 1967, but died of cancer May 5 of that year, before the new Mollie Butler Lodge was completed. Rue Kimball operated the lodge for a while, then sold to Harry and Barbara Petroff in 1974. According to a newspaper article, somewhere during this period Greer's first bar sign went up inviting people for "Cocktails in Aunt Molly's Lodge." One of her relatives felt Mollie would have issued no such invitation and prevailed upon the owner to take the sign down.[13]

Sometimes people tore into old places by choice, but many cabins and lodges burned through the years with little way to put them out except by bucket-brigade. The main part of Jokake burned during the forties—The molten plate glass windows poured out on the ground, but guests threw out furniture and office records, and Evans soon had it rebuilt to the same specifications. Turners' lodge (formerly Thompsons' place) burned in 1952. By consensus, the best thing to do was "to get out of there and let them burn." One fellow remembered a cabin fire where the lady was panicked—She very carefully handed out some clothes and pillows, then ran back in and threw all the dishes out the door!

In 1970 the Greer Fire Department (GFD) was organized. They later acquired a jeep and trailer furnished by the State Forestry Division and $800 for a pump and tank, paid for by GFD members. The people of Greer donated the money, materials, land, and labor for the fire house. Additional funds came from the various fund-raisers staged by the ladies. Through the years some twenty men and six or seven junior firemen, all volunteers, worked with equipment begged, borrowed, or bought from any place it was to be found—a little like fighting a battle with equipment from three or four different world wars! In difficult, often steep terrain the department could depend on backup from the Springerville Fire Department (thirty or forty minutes away); and the USFS for water and equipment—and manpower, when the fire threatened USFS land. The Forest Service maintained a fire warehouse at the Greer ranger station and operated a fire tanker crew out of there, but none of this was available in the winter, and in summer might be tied up on other fires.

Two forest fires, one on Escudilla Mountain near Alpine in 1951 that burned 19,500 acres, and the Greer Fire in 1971 that burned 4,300 acres, were as close to home and as serious as anyone cared to see them get. Extensive reforestation on the Greer burn by the Forest Service was "nipped in the bud" by deer, elk, mice, and chipmunks who through the years developed quite an appetite for the thousands of seedlings the USFS had planted.[14]

When it came to forest fires, the USFS "wasn't too dern bad" as far as one Greer resident was concerned. But when it came to having the Greer school house removed from the knoll in the 1960s, that wasn't very kindly received. The USFS explained that when a place on forest land outlived its usefulness, or when the use ceased to exist, then after a given time the improvements had to be removed. The USFS traditionally has not seen itself as an instrument for preservation of historical sites (as some would wish). There were later rumors that the Schultz-Lone Wolf cabin, which fell into Forest Service hands, didn't meet OSHA (Occupational Safety and Health Act of 1970) standards, and might be the next to go.

The eighty-eight year old Indian artist handed over his grandfather Yellow Wolf's sacred otter skin medicine to his adopted son, Paul Dyck (Arizona artist and student of Indian ways), and died several weeks later in 1970. The ashes of the irascible old warrior who said he avoided civilization whenever possible, were buried in his uncle Last Rider's grave—flanked by four coup sticks with eagle feathers and the flowers of the Montana prairie that extended to the majestic Rockies.[15]

But the seventies found the remote picturebook village taking on a new image and "civilization" breaking across its frontier with increasing momentum. The boast was once "fifty in winter, five-hundred in summer!" Later (in 1979) the best estimate was 150 in winter and as many as 3,000 in summer.

Being the closest town to the downhill skiing at Sunrise on the Apache Indian Reservation, and itself boasting a cross-country ski course (developed in co-operation with the USFS in 1975), people flocked into Greer whatever the season—into the village that used to be snowed in for weeks at a time. By the late 1970s, people took up residence in some 500 privately owned cabins (including thirty-eight on USFS land); 1,000 individual accommodations for rental, and 300 self-owned trailers; ate and drank at six different lodges; bought food and various other items at four or five different stores; and in the summer swelled USFS camping facilities by a count of 41,400 visitor days (in 1978).[16]

The summer of Greer's centennial year, 1979, the last of Ellis Whitney's children passed away in Eagar within a month of one another: Rebecca Wiltbank Burgess at 87, and Hyrum Wiltbank at 94.

The generation that cleared the way, sowed the seeds, produced the energy, laid down its plows and plans, took off its aprons, resigned and often content to let those younger ones have a go at it.

92

Crosby's Store

VI

Growing Old Gracefully
vs.
Staying Young Forever

On a warm fourteenth of June, 1979 the Old Lady decided to celebrate her one-hundredth birthday. You might think at *her age* she'd be cabin-bound, tending to her rheumatism and behaving herself as befitted an over-age-and-grade centenarian. But no, she decided to have a parade with flags and carts; wagons, horses and cars. It started at the Greer Lodge, barely began to get organized by the time it passed the fire station, then "got in step" with itself as it made the curve through the meadow (still refusing to look like a city street); passed the barn; negotiated the cattle guard; passed the post office (where some were still determined to get their mail, parade or no parade); and Crosby's Store; passed the "square house" and the rest of Butlers' Lodge (where there were still people sitting on the porch reviewing the parade); on to the crest of the hill, passed the glassy, sightless stare of the windows in the empty Cliff Wentz house; on down to Afton Wiltbank's where people were still leaning on the porch posts, waiting (but not for the mail to come in as they had for some thirty years).

At the head of the parade was Vince Butler—the sky-blue eyes were still a match with the tow-headed boy in pictures—weathered, experienced, "born to the saddle." ("My dad used to make me go bareback, 'specially in the winter, because that'd keep me warm—no saddle, no nothing—just throw me on a horse....")[1] Within the ranks were Jack Slade looking fine in his chariot—the metal slightly battered from Round Valley rodeos—drawn by horses nervous over kids cracking popcorn, popping balloons, and the cannon pointing over the meadow toward the east fork road, that exploded into smoke and deafening noise upon request; and George and Flossie Crosby with some of their children, grandchildren, perhaps even great-grandchildren. Afton Wiltbank, the oldest still in residence, and Mae Wiltbank, a seventy-nine year old native, were driving in a Chevrolet with open sun roof. Erma Burk was there—the new, and not-so-new of the village and vicinity—all showing their stuff.

And at the end Vince's black horse, shrouded to match, with boots pointed backwards in the stirrups, was being led, riderless—a tribute to John Wayne, American folk hero, who had died the first of that week.

And not far up the line, a new wobbly colt tied to a wagon, close to its mama—strained toward the moment of its freedom.

The Old Gal may have just wanted to have her picture taken. A Phoenix television camera crew was there trying to film the feature for the evening news, while local women with clipboards and men from horseback leaned over, down instructing, "Now be sure to mention that [so-and-so] was ... [and] I don't want you to miss...." The crew managed to remain benevolent though the look of I-do-this-seven-days-a-week lent an impressive professional boredom to their faces. They transacted an amazing amount of "business" from their station wagon.

For a moment one could almost imagine things were about the same—the old places were waiting to be taken up again; the old timers were still there, still trying to see to it things went right; that Aunt Mollie was standing on her porch, apron blowing, arm akimbo, hand square on her hip, squinting down toward the barn, trying to determine where in the world that soul had gone off to; that there were still too-small kids for too-huge horses pulling up to the store for a pop and candy bar, hoping that maybe some omniscient person would reach over the counter and porch to hand it to them so they wouldn't have to shin down to the stir-

John Cleveland and Litton Wildbank
Home and Cellar

rups, then the long way to the ground; that another barefoot boy was laying on his stomach on the little sagging bridge over the ditch in front of
Wiltbanks' and floating his twig ships to sea; and perhaps a little girl with
golden braids, half gone behind the meadow's tall grass, was gathering up
a bouquet with one of every kind to proudly present to her mother.

Later on that weekend there was a program over at the USFS amphi-
theater, site of the old Greer school house. Lot Burk, winter science
teacher, summer USFS naturalist, gathered together the various compo-
nents of the program with experience and determination, though he
wasn't able to rescue the participants' voices which were blown off to the
north by violent winds before they ever reached the audience.

There was an upright piano in a long horsetrailer parked "off-stage"
to accompany the sprinkling of songs; and awards for distinctions, accom-
plishments past and present. The pioneers reminisced from lawn chairs
by the horsetrailer and there was another good-hearted, if indecisive, argument about who had danced the most miles in the old school house—
Once they reached the upper limits of their number system, that ended
the argument. Some had the microphone brought to them at their seats,
but Mae Wiltbank had a poem by her late husband to read and wasn't
going to sit down to do it:

FIRESIDE MEMORIES

Do the grasses still grow tall in the Lee Valley
When summer rains have washed the meadow clean?
Do the birds still build their nests among the willows
When the aspen leaves have turned the hillsides green?

Do the folks still gather at Aunt Mollies
To spend winters long and cold but pleasant hours?
Does the smoke still hover round the tree tops
As it did when I was there to light the fires?

Does "Unk" still beat the dudes at pitch and poker?
Does the cakes "Af" bake still taste as good?
Does Cliff still excel at fishing stories,
and Julian spend his time a getting wood?

Have I asked you friend about Jack and Rusty?
Tell me please about Flossie, George and Fred.
Does Milt still wash Althea's dishes?
Do Gillespie's live the life they've always led?

Tell me friend have you been there lately;
If you have I sure would like to know
If Autumn paints the hills with frosty fingers
And if Angels leave their footprints in the snow.[2]

—Milo Wiltbank

The flags are down now, the poems folded and tucked into drawers full of memories, the poke bonnets hung on hooks, older honored guests helped to the cars and whisked away by relatives and friends—hoping for another day and time when people would remember them and care about the way it used to be. They're not the only ones who find solace in yesterdays. But blurred eyes and proudly beating hearts don't long obscure, silence the century-old diatribe on the use of the land and who has "any business" to make those decisions—an argument that was begun when the second guy tried to figure out how to get 'round the first guy being there before him; went through the early days of the Forest Reserves which a Flagstaff editor (in 1898) called "a fiendish piece of business;"[3] attacked the State Game and Fish Commission; all regulations by anyone; federal handouts; talk of planning and zoning and health restrictions; fences and permits and fees and fines of any kind.

The Old Lady's growing fat—feeding herself on more and more of everything; filling up all her vacant spaces; nearly bursting the seams of her britches. She assures everyone it's safe because there's a limit to her "growth." She can only go so far—the United States Forest Service owns the rest and will keep her within bounds, a kind of benevolent federally-funded girdle for individuals who can't control themselves.

The facts in the situation are these:

> Apache County contains 7.15 million acres, runs more than 200 miles long and 50 miles wide, with less than 20 percent of the land privately owned. The Indians comprise about 75 percent of its population and over 60 percent of the county's land is within the Navajo and Apache Reservations. [*White Mountain NavApache Independent*, Feb. 22, 1979]

Man, all I want to do is get away from it all. Don't give me any of your flush toilets, trash cans with lids and plastic liners, and bulletin boards with enough regulations to befuddle you into thinking they're important. Just give me a little clump of pines off the beaten path and I'm happy. Let those other suckers line up in the campground like some vacation park-and-swap—That's not my idea of a vacation.

> During the summer of 1979 the USFS expanded Hoyer Campground, formerly with a capacity of 100 people, to a capacity of approximately 300 campers. This enabled the Forest Service to concentrate all camping in one place. The Old Greer Campground to the east of the valley was closed, plowed, and reseeded. (Charles Shields, Springerville Ranger District, Apache-Sitgreaves National Forest).

Well, you can say what you want to about the Forest Service. But I'm telling you, if they didn't own most of the land around here there wouldn't be anything to call 'forest' left. The rest'd be all

97

cleared and developed, built on. Heck, these fields used to be all grain and potatoes. Now they're taking 40, 60, 80 acres of farmland and planting a house every acre or so and pretty soon there won't be any fields or meadows to look down on or across at all. Trouble is, people are still trying to live off the land—off selling it.

They appreciated it in this way: It was here; it was wonderful; it was God's country and all that; and they was satisfied to leave it as it was.

The people are the only ones who can put the brakes on (the growth). The pressure of people wanting to buy lots up there has been tremendous. The local people have resisted to some extent. That little valley can only support so many people and the more people you have the more pollution you'll have. I would have thought if they could keep more open space—and they should keep all the open space they can now. If they're going to have more summer people it should be done more on a lodge-type basis, concentrated. What I hate to see happen is cabins all over the place, on the hillsides. 'Course, when I started going there, there were just a few places, hardly anyone went to a cabin. Wiltbanks had about the only rentals. Everybody camped.

The local people just lived kind of from day to day. They were so damned busy just trying to stay alive and keep the bank paid that they'd talk about it: 'Gee, we'd like to do this, build a bigger place over here ... Boy, let's sit down, this thing could really develop; let's get a master plan and let's do all these things. . . .' Things just grew by helter skelter and most everybody just left everyone else alone to some extent.

I hope people design what they build to fit into the environment. What really irritates me is to see trailers of all colors all over the valley. I think trailers are the thing that seem to change the appearance of the valley more than anything else.

I really don't feel entirely one way or another. I can't stand seeing a bunch of junk around, but it just kills my soul to see all the old places torn down and cleared away. Nothing is more fun than poking around, exploring, sort of getting into the way it used to be. I believe we need regulations and all that—but let's just not sterilize the place.

The most serious problem is the sewage disposal. There's been some talk of developing a sewage system and requiring that everyone use it. Possibly just in the interest of plain health they should, or maybe will, limit the housing.

Well to me, the Forest Service then—We had to have it, I think. Today they're getting it down that it's not any good. They're making so many laws that the people who have lived here all their lives—if you go up and you have to go to the bathroom and you go behind a tree, they fine you, you see. Now people have been all over that mountain and you *have* to go to the bathroom; you can't just always go to one of theirs they have in certain places, 'cause you're not near it.

Well, I told him he'd better do something about his sewage. 'Course, he could care less. You'd never find him getting down wind of the situation.

Gosh, I can't see the place's changed at all. What's changed is the people—All the oldtimers have either passed away or moved away.

The other day this friend of mine and I were poking around an old garbage dump and found some really neat old whiskey and medicine bottles. We divied up our 'treasures' fair and square. Later on that same day I was walking toward Government Springs and noticed with disgust the beer bottles thrown along the road. Then I wondered, 'Will someone in 75-100 years think our garbage is quaint—our Michelob-browns and Heineken-greens a real find?'

When I came back here I just couldn't stand the drinkin' and things like that that was going on. The way the people were—you know what I mean. I just didn't like that—you know how that sort of thing causes friction.

Well, you have to be realistic.

The only similarity between Greer then and now is the name.

Uncle Snap liked to drink whiskey and fish and hunt—most delightful guy you've ever met in your life. He'd stay up there all summer on the stream with a case of whiskey, and he didn't give a damn for the game warden or the game laws. He said, 'By God, the good Lord put those fish in that creek and no tin-star son-of-a-bitch is going to tell me how many of 'em I'm going to catch.'

Our population growth in the state so far has been almost entirely in the big towns. In the future I think you're going to see a tremendous growth in little towns. The pressure on wildlife is going to be much greater than it has been in the past.' Course it's been awfully high in the past few years because of the four-wheel drive, which you can drive anywhere in the back country and they've done it. They've cut up the country with roads.

There will have to be more regulations to protect wildlife during the breeding season and seasons of reproduction. When the turkey are nesting, the elk, deer, and antelope are dropping fawns and calves—the wildlife is going to have to have more protection than it's getting. When you have people moving into these areas you have to have more management of wildlife, control of predators. The food supply and remoteness are both suffering and wildlife requires at certain times remoteness. When the deer are dropping their fawns, they just won't reproduce good if they can't find places to hide their fawns and the same is true of elk and their calves—It's their nature. And if they can't find a place to go to, to

99

have their fawns where they can secrete them, they'll quit having them.

They used to have a big old turkey trap down there, you know. Everybody'd used it. It was a lean-to, sort of covered. The turkey would go in there to get the grain and they couldn't find their way out.

The idea of the Greer Refuge as I recall it, was to keep people from hunting turkey around there 'cause all the people really liked to see those turkey come wandering in there in the summertime. I can think of no other real reason for setting up a refuge in that area except as a turkey refuge because other wildlife didn't use it that much. There were too many people in there.

When we first got there, there was no season on fishing, no season on hunting, no season on nothing. But then they began to have to put it on. When they began dishing it out, the people couldn't hardly take it. They didn't abuse the land—There wasn't that many there. But now it's abused terribly and they're killing off all the turkey, deer, antelope—everything. When I was a kid, they were so plentiful. We'd catch and kill only what we needed—It wasn't wasted.

Hell, this place would starve to death, fold up, and blow away if it weren't for the tourists and people coming in—building cabins and stuff. I think we'll just keep growing till we can't grow anymore. The more the better, far's I'm concerned. It's good for business.

I think it's a quaint little place; people are very nice. It's a place to get away for a short period of time—something a little different. Literally, I think it's a nice vacation spot. I wouldn't want to be there too long, because there isn't enough to do. I don't see it's developed that much. Of course you've got to have someplace to go. You wouldn't want it to be like what's happened the last 30-40 years in Phoenix where you can hardly drive down the street.

Our plains are stocked with thousands of cattle, horses and sheep and still there is room for more . . . Young men look well to your rights and if Uncle Sam owes you 160 or 1,000 acres, see that you get it. [*Holbrook Times*, May 17, 1884]

You can have it this month for $10,000 an acre—Next month it goes up to $13,000. Take it or leave it, of course. But frankly, I wouldn't advise waiting too long.

We just used the land as to what we could best use it for. Even though it be a small piece, we'd plow it under and plant a patch of potatoes and something of this nature.

So what does this 'saturation thing' mean? That every available piece of land will be used either for a cabin, a trailer, or commercial development—and it'll be saturated all right. It'll reach the point where the land won't be able to take anymore. It won't be able to take any more people, any more vehicles, any more of

*their waste, either human or their garbage—Then at what point
do we realize we've gone too far? Once you've gone too far, it's
hard to pull back. No one's going to give up a freedom they're
used to having.*

Boy, they are really paranoid—always witch hunting. There's no
problem I tell you. Some people just aren't happy unless they're
bitching about something, poking around, stirring up a hornet's
nest.

*It's my land and what I do on it or with it, far's that is con-
cerned, is no one's gol-durned business.*

So we think we're important—just look at those stars! [The 'clos-
ing argument' proposed on a summer evening's walk, which
opened a new line of thought.]

Epilogue

In 1911, L. C. Hughes who had been governor of the Arizona Territory, 1893-1896, became somewhat transported in speaking of the pioneer-type:

> Character is the result of observation, especially of physical surroundings. Behold these conditions in lowering mountains, illimitable plains, mighty canyons, gorges, and other natural phenomena! Behold a land of vitalizing and never-ceasing sunshine; the torrential rains with unprecedented lightning and thunder; the heavenly scenery of the night! All of which awaken and inspire imagination, love, and adoration for the sublime and beautiful, the sentiment resulting therefrom assimilated in the development of the character of man. Of such is the citizenship of Arizona's stalwart pioneer and their offspring. *(The Earth: The Santa Fe Southwest,* Chicago, April, 1911)

That may have been believable then, but no one can look at the polyglot of people who pass through, compose a "pioneer" village like Greer and not realize the difficulty, impossibility of describing who's here and why.

Everyone is coming from a different place—"a whole new breed of cat," and some just a remodel of older styles. Sometimes looking at a few of the people in one of the local bars one wonders: "Where in the heck did they come from and why are they *here*?" "They" don't look like fishermen-women, don't look like they're in the market for land, don't look like tourists. They're part of the U.S. scene one sees everywhere. How would one describe them? They're young, they're itinerants—but not "hippies," that's obsolete. They might come on motorcycles, but not necessarily. They have money to spend—They buy a steak dinner and a bottle of wine; they play pool and the jukebox. They drink beer, but they drink mixed drinks too.

They're like an instant generation—They just appeared out of nowhere. They don't know where they're going, but don't really care. They don't seem to have any background, any heritage they'd speak of; don't come from a particular piece of goods. They're not interested in much of anything; but casually interested in almost everything. They end up here—lingering on the bar stools, hunched over the cue sticks. Where do they stay? Where do they belong? Maybe nowhere, maybe everywhere. They cruise through and cruise out.

Where are all the old faces? Do they keep to themselves now? And what of that? Everyone used to do things together, so they said anyway. People used to have picnics, fish-fries, dances, and there were always sort of gathering places—might be the post office down at the Wiltbanks'. One was sure to bump into ten different people one knew as they crowded into the tiny room trying to get in the mail line or to their boxes—or at Butlers' or Crosby's Store. But now the action is at the bars for some of the people; and the old ones are sitting behind closed doors. It would take a statistician with x-ray vision to know how many people are in the valley and who they are and what they do and what they think. Maybe people just want to be left alone—who knows?

Sometimes the younger ones look at the older ones and say with more than a slight edge of disgust, "What a red-neck!" They're part of the "macho scene" that arrive in four-wheel drives built so high you could use a sports car as trundle bed under them. Between their headlights and CB antennas they look like chrome-plated bugs ready to crawl up, down, and over the countryside. There's invariably a rifle or two on the rack, back of the cab; and a handgun or two under the seat, in the glove compartment; maybe a six-pack. They're from "KJ Country" (country radio station KJJJ-Phoenix); out to prove themselves, and use the land to do it. There seems to be a need to subdue, to kill; a kind of barrel-chested bravado that seeks a trophy (They don't really need the meat.)—people who measure their fish, mount their kill, and stick a feather in their cap. The more paraphernalia, the more visible, the more clout they have.

Then there are those who come in with money, buy up all the land—at any price. They can afford the luxury of deciding what it is they want to do with it. And if they decide to do nothing with it, they can do that too. They're the ones who build all-redwood, cantilevered "cabins" on mountainsides no one in their right mind would build on; look down through huge thermo-pane windows on the "settlers," somehow figuring a way to write the whole venture off as "business expense." Do they put the residents down?—these people who are trying to make a living off the season which still isn't quite twelve months a year, at least not twelve months doing the same thing. These people come in and lord it over everybody—throw their money and weight around, make demands. They're new too. But then most everyone is.

The "wilderness-freak" just pleads for everyone to do nothing: Leave it as if no human being had ever come this way before—no garbage; no fires; no soap in the stream; no rearranging of rocks, wood, or duff; no noise; no firearms or violence; no alcohol; no groups over four; no short-cuts; no off-road vehicles; no going-behind-trees. They hike over the mountains, go to elaborate means to erase their tracks, and blanch white, even gag at the idea of meat and beds and suitcases—If it can't be done in cut-offs, out of a backpack, fueled by granola, it's not worth doing. And if one is not careful, the Sierra Club or some other subversive group will grab some perfectly good land and put it into a newly-proposed wilderness. One must be alert for this kind of thing all the time.

If there is a common-denominator, a level of distillation, it may be the combination in each of John Wayne-Alice-in-Wonderland-Jacob Hamblin-Mollie Butler and a little bit of Lone Wolf thrown in for flair and spice. Everyone is searching for his-her kind of adventure, and the kind of grit, guts, and imagination to recognize it when one comes upon it. It involves a new place, a new way of living—a chance to explore, to try something one has never tackled before, not always with an end in mind; to try a new approach, make a new track.

There's enough cowboy-girl in each to search for frontiers where there's freedom to set out on one's own; start a new venture; build a new building, however small; plow a plot, plant a garden; make a new conquest; explore never-known parts of the land, of oneself.

The modern day dilemma is, it doesn't *have* to be done—It's not as if anyone was on a mission, with a kind of do-or-die directive sending him or her on to superhuman feats of physical endurance and accomplishment. Sometimes the boredom, purposelessness, thrill-seeking with which people now approach their recreation, diversions seem a twisted motivation compared to the pioneers': They didn't do things just because they were bored, because it might be fun, so much as they needed to be done. There seemed to be a reason-ableness to what and why they did things, and where they went to do them.

Or—perhaps not. It may be that a lot of people who set out for the West were itchy, rootless wanderers who felt constricted, felt like they were at a dead end; whose boundless confidence was based on little but a good imagination and agile tongue. It may be that some, but not all, who went on colonizing missions were misfits; needed to be shifted around; were on the list to be relocated; to be demoted, to be taken down a peg or two. Who can say?

If one doesn't have to do it, why is it important still? If one can't entirely play the child again, have the riotous good times, the anything-I-want-to-do times; if one can't cut down any tree; tap any source of water; throw garbage out of immediate sight; and direct human waste out the open end of a pipe headed downhill without going through a lot of hassle and red tape, is it worth it? If one can't even sit back and relax with a glass of cool Rocky Mountain spring water without giving a flickering thought about amoebas, maybe the experience is not all one thought it might be.

Yet there are still logs to play "follow the leader on," to wobble across the stream with fishing pole and all one's gear; still sharp rocks to test one's foot against in an icy, rushing stream; still terrifying thunderstorms to shudder at and lightning bolts to humble one; and men who ride the range with ropes coiled on their saddles with weathered faces and Stetsons mottled with sweat; wood stoves to manage; forests to be tramped, mountains to top; berries to be picked; petals to be counted off. There is beauty to feast the eyes and feed the soul—that catches the breath and stops the heart.

At the same time there are hard problems to face and deal with that won't dissolve under massive doses of sentimentality and "rear-view vision."

One of the greatest threats to the "slight edge" of excitement some are looking for—the thing that really flattens and dulls the possibilities—is man's predilection for comfort, safety, and sameness. A buttoned-down mentality doesn't recognize the frontier—never really "gets into it."

And there might just be something in the idea that it's not absolutely necessary to take, to own, to "improve," to plunder what was ours in the first place—freely given, to explore and enjoy.

Chapter Notes

Chapter I.

[1] Greer Quadrangle, Arizona-Apache Co., 7.5 Minute Series (Topographic), United States Department of the Interior, Geological Survey, Denver, Colorado; Taped interview with Charles S. Shields, Recreation and Land Staff Officer, Springerville Ranger District, Apache-Sitgreaves National Forest, Springerville, Arizona, 9 March 1979.

[2] Nelson Butler, "Maverick, Arizona" (mimeographed), (Courtesy of Southwest Forest Industries, Phoenix, Arizona), 3 May 1978, pp. 1-3, 8-9.

[3] Apache-Sitgreaves National Forests, "Recreational Opportunities" (USDA, Forest Service, Southwestern Region, 1979), p. 5.

[4] James Willard Schultz, *In the Great Apache Forest: The Story of a Lone Boy Scout* (Boston: Houghton Mifflin Company, 1920), p. 121.

[5] *Ibid.*, pp. 18, 20.

[6] Ryan Reinhold, "Mt. Baldy," *White Mountains of Arizona* (1978): pp. 52, 93.

[7] Will C. Barnes, rev. and enl. by Byrd H. Granger, *Arizona Place Names* (Tucson: The University of Arizona Press, 1960), p. XIV; Atella Haws, Milo Wiltbank, Twylah Hamblin, comp., *Eagar Ward, St. Johns Stake: Church of Jesus Christ of Latter Day Saints: Dedicatory Service* (6 May 1951), p. 5. Hereinafter cited: Eagar Ward, *Dedicatory Service.*

[8] James O. Pattie, *Personal Narrative of James O. Pattie of Kentucky* (Cincinnati: John H. Wood, 1831; reprint edit., Vol. XVIII, *Early Western Travels: 1748-1846*, ed. Reuben Gold Thwaites, Cleveland: Arthur H. Clark Company, 1905), p. 130; Barnes, *Arizona Place Names*, p. 5.

[9] Fred Winn, "The Apache National Forest" (mimeographed), Fred Winn Collection. Tucson: Arizona Historical Society Library, pp. 7-8. Hereinafter cited: AHS.

[10] Dan R. Williamson, "Al Sieber, Famous Scout of the Southwest," *Arizona Historical Review* (January, 1931), pp. 61-62.

[11] Patrick Hamilton, Arizona Immigration Commissioner in 1884, "Arizona—An Historical Outline," *Arizona Historical Review* (April, 1928), pp. 29-30.

[12] Barnes, *Arizona Place Names*, p. 233.

[13] Bert Haskett, "Early History of the Cattle Industry in Arizona," *Arizona Historical Review* (October, 1935), p. 18.

[14] Martha Summerhayes, *Vanished Arizona: Recollections of My Army Life* (Philadelphia: J.B. Lippincott Company, 1908; reprint edit., Philadelphia: J.B. Lippincott Company, 1963), p. 80.

[15] Roscoe G. Willson, "Arizona Days: In Arizona's Hayday," *Arizona Republic*, Phoenix, 24 June 1979.

[16] Barnes, *Arizona Place Names*, pp. 3-4.

Chapter II.

[1] Eagar Ward, *Dedicatory Service*, p. 4.

[2] Winn, "The Apache National Forest," AHS, p. 1.

[3] Charles S. Peterson, *Take Up Your Mission: Mormon Colonizing Along the Little Colorado River, 1870-1900* (Tucson: The University of Arizona Press, 1973), p. 164.

[4] Haskett, "Early History of the Cattle Industry in Arizona," p. 26.

[5] Richard J. Hinton, *The Handbook to Arizona: Its Resources, History, Towns, Mines, Ruins and Scenery* (San Francisco: Payot, Upham & Co., 1878; reprint edit., Tucson: Arizona Silhouettes, 1954), pp. ix-x.

[6] Telephone interview with E. C. Becker, Springerville, Arizona, 15 July 1979; Ben Avery, "Spanish Settler Begins Community's Growth," *Arizona Republic*, 6 July 1952; Bert Haskett, "History of the Sheep Industry in Arizona," *Arizona Historical Review* (July, 1936), p. 19; Levi S. Udall, Arizona Supreme Court Justice, "Gustav Becker, Springerville-Memorial Day Address," Springerville, 30 May 1948, Phoenix: Department of Library, Archives and Public Records, State Capitol Building. Hereinafter cited: LAPR.

[7] Eagar Ward, *Dedicatory Service*, p. 6; Winn, "The Apache National Forest," AHS, pp. 1-3.

[8] *Ibid.*, pp. 3-4; "History of Highways Going to Springerville" (reprint of statement by Julius W. Becker, made at request of Arizona State Highway Department, ca. 1953), *White Mountain Roundup*, Springerville, 3 July 1970.

[9] "Eliza Catherine Rudd Tells of Early History," *White Mountain Roundup*, 3 July 1970.

[10] "History of Highways," *White Mountain Roundup.*

[11] Eagar Ward, *Dedicatory Service*, p. 8; Telephone interview with E. C. Becker.

[12] Thomas Howell Hamblin, "Pioneer Tells of Hardships" (newspaper article, n.d., n.p.), LAPR.

[13] Peterson, *Take Up Your Mission*, p. 66.

[14] *Ibid.*, p. 85.

[15] Jay Wagoner, *Arizona's Heritage* (Santa Barbara: Peregrine Smith, Inc., 1977), p. 197.

[16] Spencer Watson Wiltbank's children who accompanied him in 1880: George, Frank, Minah, Ted, and daughter and son-in-law, Ann and William W. Lund.

[17] Eagar Ward, *Dedicatory Service*, p. 7.

[18] Roberta Clayton, "Pioneer Women of Navajo County," Unpublished manuscript, Mesa; Arizona Branch, Genealogical Library [LDS].

[19] Hamblin, "Pioneer Tells of Hardships," LAPR.

[20] Taped interview with Ben Avery, Phoenix, Arizona, 26 February 1979.

[21] Haskett, "Early History of the Cattle Industry," pp. 3, 37.

Chapter III.

¹ Taped interview with Afton Haws Wiltbank (Mrs. John Cleveland), Tucson, Arizona, 28 February 1979.

² Peterson, *Take Up Your Mission,* pp. 163-4.

³ Taped interview with Ed G. Dentzer Jr., Phoenix, Arizona, 26 February 1979.

⁴ Letter from William J. Buehler, President: White Mountain Historical Society, Springerville, to Karen M. Applewhite, 8 May 1979.

⁵ "Manuscript History of Greer Ward," Salt Lake City: Archives, LDS Church Historical Department; Some feel "Lee Valley" was named after the Richard Lee family mentioned in the "Manuscript History of Greer Ward"; others, that it was named after Willard Lee and his wife Lucinda, who lived there for several years.

⁶ Barnes, *Arizona Place Names,* p. 239.

⁷ Letter from Sylvester Hale to John Butler, n.d. (Courtesy of Vince Butler, South Fork, Springerville).

⁸ Taped interview with Afton Wiltbank.

⁹ Telephone interview with William B. Thompson, Pasadena, California, 16 May 1979.

¹⁰ Peterson, *Take Up Your Mission,* p. 36.

¹¹ Taped interview with Mae Hale Wiltbank (Mrs. Milo), Mesa, Arizona, 21 March 1979.

¹² Letter from E. R. DeWitt, St. Johns, Arizona, to John Butler (Courtesy of Vince Butler, South Fork, Springerville), 15 January 1937; Taped interview with Mae Hale Wiltbank.

¹³ John O. Hall Family Papers, n.d. (Courtesy of Laverl Hall, St. Johns, Arizona).

¹⁴ Taped interview with Mae Hale Wiltbank.

¹⁵ George H. Crosby Jr., "As My Memory Recalls: The Hashknife Outfit," *St. Johns Observer,* 1 March 1924.

¹⁶ "History of Highways," *White Mountain Roundup.*

¹⁷ Becker Family Collection, AHS.

¹⁸ Rod Bender, *Field Guide to Fishing* (Phoenix: Arizona Recreational Publications), p. 7.

¹⁹ Hall Family Papers.

²⁰ Eagar Ward, *Dedicatory Service,* p. 29.

²¹ DeWitt letter.

²² Barnes, *Arizona Place Names,* p. 4, explains, "Benny and Rosey Creeks, lying side by side, memorialize a romance which didn't materialize. Prior to 1900 Rosey Thompson was set to marry Benny Howell, or so he thought, but while he was away getting the license, she ran off with Fred Hoffman and married him."

²³ Effie May Butler Wiltbank Papers, AHS.

[24] "Manuscript History of Greer Ward" [LDS].

[25] Mollie Butler Life Sketch, LAPR.

[26] Willmirth DeWitt tape, Milo Wiltbank Collection, AHS, St. Johns, 1957.

[27] Remarks by Sally Howell Brown, Show Low, Arizona, Greer Reunion, 15 June 1979.

[28] Effie May Butler Wiltbank Papers, AHS.

[29] Telephone interview with Atella Wiltbank Haws (Mrs. Carl), Eagar, Arizona, 19 June 1979.

[30] Effie May Butler Wiltbank Papers, AHS.

[31] Taped interview with Mae Hale Wiltbank.

[32] Mollie Butler Life Sketch, LAPR.

[33] Willmirth DeWitt tape, AHS.

[34] Effie May Butler Wiltbank Papers, AHS.

[35] Remarks by Irl Lund, Eagar, Arizona, Greer Reunion, 15 June 1979.

Chapter IV.

[1] DeWitt letter.

[2] Taped interview with Mae Hale Wiltbank.

[3] John A. Hamblin, *Heritage: A Personal History* (Mesa: Emby Originals, 1977), pp. 23-24.

[4] *Ibid.*, p. 24.

[5] Schultz, *In the Great Apache Forest, p. 3.*

[6] Taped interview with Mae Hale Wiltbank.

[7] *Ibid.;* Recipe for Cele Hamblin's salt rising bread (as remembered by Mae Wiltbank): "[Cele Hamblin would] get up, take a handful of cornmeal, put it in a little bucket, pour boiling water over it, maybe a little salt, set it on the hearth of the cook stove. After breakfast she'd put some flour in—maybe a handful or two of graham flour, a little sugar, salt, a teaspoon of soda. The stuff would rise—stink. By noon we had big loaves of bread—delicious with green onions, watercress, and milk."

[8] Remarks by Buzz Haws, Eagar, Arizona, Greer Reunion, 15 June 1979.

[9] Taped interview with Atella Wiltbank Haws, Eagar, Arizona, 7 March 1979.

[10] Winn, "The Apache National Forest," AHS, p. 5.

[11] M. Alice Berry Patterson, "Apache County's Immense Wealth of Forest," *Arizona Magazine* (August, 1911), p. 9.

[12] George Fitzpatrick and Edwin A. Tucker, *Men Who Matched the Mountains: The Forest Service in the Southwest* (United States Department of Agriculture, Forest Service, Western Division, 1972), pp. 85-86.

[13] *Ibid.*, p. 31.

[14] *Ibid.*, p. 75.

[15] Wagoner, *Arizona's Heritage,* p. 240.

[16] Winn, "The Story of Lee Valley and Greer," *Arizona Cattlelog* (July, 1969), pp. 18-19.

[17] Winn, "The Great Apache Forest," AHS, pp. 10-11.

[18] *Arizona Republic,* 6 July 1952; Albert J. Levine, *From Indian Trails to Jet Trails* (Snowflake Historical Society, 1977), p. 52.

[19] Taped interview with Ed G. Dentzer Jr.

[20] "History of Highways," *White Mountain Roundup.*

[21] Becker Family Collection, AHS.

[22] Victor H. Dittmar, "At 89, Ed Becker Retires—Just a Little," *White Mountain Independent,* Springerville, 24 April 1979.

[23] James Willard Schultz and Dr. T. J. Bouldin, "A Few Facts About Apache County," St. Johns: St. Johns Observer Printers, November, 1915.

[24] "Blackfeet Man: James Willard Schultz," *Montana Heritage Series,* No. 12, Montana Historical Society, 1961.

[25] Taped interview with Ed G. Dentzer Jr.; Lone Wolf tape, Milo Wiltbank Collection, AHS, Greer, ca. 1956.

[26] Taped interview with Cora Gibbons Sharp (Mrs. Clair), Shumway, Arizona, 14 April 1979.

[27] Telephone interview with William B. Thompson.

[28] Taped interview with Mae Hale Wiltbank.

[29] George Wharton James, *Arizona the Wonderland* (Boston: The Page Co., 1917), pp. 141-2.

[30] Taped interview with Milt Coggins Sr., Phoenix, Arizona, 21 April 1979.

[31] Telephone interview with G. R. Carlock, Phoenix, Arizona, 3 May 1979.

[32] Taped interview with Ed G. Dentzer Jr.

[33] *Ibid.*

[34] Fred Winn was Supervisor of Apache National Forest (1914-18) and retired from the USFS as Supervisor, Coronado National Forest (1943). He was quite deaf from an iceboat accident in his youth; while his wife had an operatic voice that could be heard clear across the meadow when she was practicing in the Greer school house!

[35] Taped interview with Ed G. Dentzer Jr.

[36] Taped interview with Fritzie Struckmeyer Ryley (Mrs. Francis J.), Phoenix, Arizona, 17 April 1979.

[37] Mollie Butler Life Sketch, LAPR.

[38] Taped interview with Katherine Coffin Decker (Mrs. Harold C.), Phoenix, Arizona, 22 February 1979.

[39] Telephone interview with William B. Thompson; Taped interview with Vince Butler, South Fork, Springerville, Arizona, 8 March 1979.

[40] Taped interview with Cora Sharp.

[41] *Arizona State Business Directory* (Denver: The Gazatteer Publishing & Printing Co.).

[42] Taped interview with Paul Beer, Phoenix, Arizona, 28 March 1979.

[43] Personal interview with George E. and Florence Crosby, Mesa, Arizona, 21 May 1979; Taped interview with Ed G. Dentzer Jr.

[44] Taped interview with Arthur Leeds, Greer, Arizona, 9 March 1979.

[45] Wagoner, *Arizona's Heritage,* pp. 301-2.

[46] John Butler, Notes on history of Greer, ca. 1937 (Courtesy of Vince Butler, South Fork, Springerville).

[47] Andrew Jenson, *Encyclopedic History of the Church of Jesus Christ of Latter-day Saints* (Salt Lake City: Corporation of the President of the Church [LDS], 1941), p. 305.

[48] Letter from Judith Carlock Wilder (Mrs. Carleton), Tucson, Arizona, to Karen M. Applewhite, July, 1979.

[49] Taped interview with Ed G. Dentzer Jr.

[50] Taped interview with Irl Lund, Eagar, Arizona, 7 March 1979.

[51] *Arizona Daily Star,* Tucson, 17 May 1953: Taped interview with Mary Ross Gillespie, M.D. (Mrs. Ward R.), Phoenix, Arizona, 28 March 1979.

[52] Personal interview with Denver Evans and Barbara Evans Farris, Paradise Valley, Arizona, 2 May 1979.

[53] "Fatality Is Result of Shock," *Arizona Republic,* 5 March 1940; Gustav and his brother Julius married daughters of John C. Homrighausen. Gustav married Louisa and Julius, Minnie. Julius died at age forty-five in 1893.

[54] Taped interview with Vince Butler.

Chapter V.

[1] Hall Family Papers.

[2] Taped interview with Cora Sharp.

[3] Taped interview with Paul Beer.

[4] Taped interview with Vince Butler; Taped interview with Ed G. Dentzer Jr.; Personal interview with George E. Crosby.

[5] Taped interview with Ed G. Dentzer Jr.

[6] Personal interview with Clayton Jones, Phoenix, Arizona, May, 1979.

[7] Taped interview with Mary Ross Gillespie, M.D.

[8] Taped interview with Julian Herrod, Phoenix, Arizona, 31 March 1979; Taped interview with Dean Coulter, Phoenix, Arizona, 28 March 1979.

[9] Taped interview with Arthur Leeds.

[10] Telephone interview with Donna Entrekin (Mrs. Leland), Apache Junction, Arizona, 27 April 1979.

[11] Letter from Kent Rhoton, Navopache Electric Co-Operative, Inc., Lakeside, Arizona, to Karen M. Applewhite, 22 March 1979.

[12] Taped interview with Ben Avery.

[13] Paul W. Pollock, *American Biographical Encyclopedia* (Phoenix: By the Author, 1967), Vol. I: p. 186; *White Mountain Independent,* 31 May 1979.

[14] Letter from Dan Leeds, Greer, Arizona, to Karen M. Applewhite, 26 March 1979; Taped interview with Charles Shields.

[15] Paul Dyck, "Lone Wolf Returns," *Montana: The Magazine of Western History,* Winter, 1972, pp. 18-31.

[16] Estimates by Alice Lloyd, Postmaster, Greer, Arizona, May, 1979; Greer Chamber of Commerce brochure, 1979; Taped interview with Charles Shields: According to Mr. Shields of the Springerville Ranger District, Apache-Sitgreaves Natl'l Forest, the USFS considers a "visitor day" to be one person on the site for twelve hours, or three persons on site for four hours.

Chapter VI.

[1] Taped interview with Vince Butler.

[2] Milo Wiltbank, "Fireside Memories," Composed in Greer, Arizona, 1962. Mentioned in Mr. Wiltbank's poem are "Aunt Mollie"—Mollie Butler; Unk"—John Cleveland Wiltbank; "Af"—JCW's wife, Afton Wiltbank; "Cliff"—Cliff Wentz; "Julian"—Julian Herrod; "Jack and Rusty"—son and daughter-in-law of J. C. and Afton Wiltbank; "Flossie, George"—Florence and George E. Crosby; "Fred"—Fred Burk; "Milt, Althea"—Milt and Althea Turner; "Gillespie's"—Mary Ross and Ward R. Gillespie.

[3] George Fitzpatrick and Edwin A. Tucker, *Men Who Matched the Mountains,* p. 7.

On The Road To Nowhere

Appendix

Greer Business

Arizona State Business Directory
(Denver: The Gazatteer Publishing Co.)

1912-13
Butler, Effie, banker
Butler, J. F., meat market, boots, & shoes
Butler, Mollie, bakery, postmaster
Butler, S. A., boarding house
Crosby, Hanna, artist
Crosby & Gibbons, florists
Frost, Jack, ice
Haws, Mrs. Dora, dressmaker
Wiltbank, Hyrum & Frank, barbers

1915-16
Butler, Effie, banker
Butler, J. F., meat market, boots, & shoes
Butler, Mollie, bakery, postmaster
Crosby & Gibbons, florists

(1918-19-as noted in text)

1920
Butler, Mollie, postmaster
Butler & Wiltbank, bakery
Greer, S., lumber
Jefcoat, Robt., shoemaker
Nelson, James, blacksmith
Robins, Margaret, prin. sch.
Robinson, M. G., phys.
Wiltbank, E. W., lumber

1922
Butler, John T., boarding house, carp.
Butler, Mollie, postmaster
Schultz, J. W., printer, photog.
Wiltbank, M. J., barber
Wiltbank, W. E. & Co., live Stock
Butler & Wiltbank, carp.

1914-15
Butler, Effie, banker
Butler, J. F., meat market, boots, & shoes
Butler, Mollie, bakery, postmaster
Crosby & Gibbons, florists

1916-17
Butler, Effie, banker
Butler, J. F., meat market, boots, & shoes
Butler, Mollie, bakery, postmaster
Crosby & Gibbons, florists

1921
Butler, John T., boarding house, carp.
Schultz, J. W., printer, photog.
Butler, Mollie, postmaster
Thompson Hotel
Wiltbank, M. J., barber
Wiltbank, W. E. & Co., live Stock

1923
Butler, John T., boarding house, carp.
Butler, Mollie, postmaster
Butler & Wiltbank, carpenters
Day, Henry, ice
Drew, D. C., prin. sch.
Round Valley Chamber of Commerce
Schultz, J. W., printer, photog.
Wiltbank, W. E. & Co., live Stock

(1924-25-as noted in text)

1926
Butler, John T., boarding house, carp.
Butler, Uley, barber
Butler & Wiltbank, carp. builders
Crosby, Geo. E., groc.
Lund, Marion, stage line
Peterson, Mrs. L. B., prin. sch.
Wiltbank, John C., plumber, postm.

1928
Butler, John T., carp. builder
Crosby, Geo. E., groc.
Day, Henry, sawmill
Greer Lodge (hotel), John T. Butler, prop.
Hamblin, Josephine, princ. sch.
Lund, Marion, freighter
State Fish Hatchery (Squirrel Springs)
      Theo Faunce, supt.
Wiltbank, John C., plumber, postmaster
Wiltbank, Mae, bakery

1930
Crosby, Geo. E., groc.
Day, Henry, sawmill
Greer Lodge (hotel), John T. Butler, prop.
Hall, Lucy, princ. sch.
McPhaul, E. L., ranger
State Fish Hatchery (Squirrel Springs)
      Eugene Pearson, fish culturist
Wiltbank, John C., plumber, postm.
Wiltbank, Mae, bakery

1932
Burk, Fred, sawmill
Butler, John T., contr.
Butler, Uley, barber
Crosby, Geo. E., groc., auto fil. stat.
Greer Lodge (hotel), John T. Butler, prop.
Hobson, Mrs. H. P., laundry
Newcomb, Ruth G., prin. sch.
State Fish Hatchery, Geo. R. See
Wiltbank, John C., plumber, postm.

1927
Butler, Uley, barber
Butler & Wiltbank, carp. bldg.
Crosby, Geo E., groc.
Day, Henry, sawmill
Greer Lodge (hotel), John T. Butler, prop.
Lund, Marion, freighter
Peterson, Mrs. L. B., prin. sch.
State Fish Hatchery (Squirrel Springs)
      Theo Faunce, supt.
Wiltbank, John C., plumber, postmaster

1929
Butler, John T., carp. builder
Crosby, Geo. E., groc.
Day, Henry, sawmill
Greer Lodge (hotel), John T. Butler, prop.
Hall, Lucy, princ. sch.
Lund, Marion, freighter
McPhaul, E. L., forest ranger
State Fish Hatchery (Squirrel Springs)
      Theo Faunce, supt.
Wiltbank, John C., plumber, postm.
Wiltbank, Mae, bakery

1931
Crosby, Geo. E., groc., auto fil. stat.
Greer Lodge (hotel), John T. Butler, prop.
Newcomb, Ruth G., princ. sch.
Schultz, Hart (Lone Wolf), artist
State Fish Hatchery, Eugene Pearson
Wiltbank, John C., plumber, postm.

1936
Burk, Fred, sawmill
Butler, John T., contr.
Crosby, Geo. E., groc., auto fil. stat.
Greer Lodge (hotel), John T. Butler, prop.
Schultz, Hart (Lone Wolf), artist
Wiltbank, John C., plumber, postm.

1937
Burk, Fred, sawmill
Butler, John T., contr.
Crosby, Geo. E., groc., auto fil. stat.
Day, Henry, sawmill
Greer Lodge (hotel), John T. Butler, prop.
Pahaska Lodge, J. A. Laverty, mgr.
    (7 mi. northwest)
Schultz, Hart (Lone Wolf), artist
Sharp, C. L., forest ranger

1939
Burk, Fred, sawmill
Crosby, Geo. E., groc., auto fil. stat.
Day, Henry, sawmill
Greer Lodge (hotel), John T. Butler, prop.
Hamblin, Graham, justice of the peace
Jokake Guest Ranch (B. Evans)
Oelson, Merle C., forest ranger
Wiltbank, John C., plumber, postm.

1938
Burk, Fred, sawmill
Butler, John T., contr.
Crosby, Geo. E., groc. auto fil. stat.
Day, Henry, sawmill
Greer Lodge (hotel), John T. Butler, prop.
Oleson, Merle C., forest ranger
Schultz, Hart (Lone Wolf), artist
Trammel, Connor, justice peace,
    res. Springerville
Wiltbank, John C., plumber, postm.

1941-42
Burk, Fred, sawmill
Butler, Mollie, hotel
Butler, Uley, barber
Butler, Vince, tourist guide
Crosby, Geo. E., groc., auto fil. stat.
Jokake Guest Ranch (B. Evans)
McDaniel, Henry, forest ranger
Norton, John, shingle mill
Schultz, Hart (Lone Wolf), artist
Wentz, C. B., building contractor
Wiltbank, John C., plumber, postm.
Woods, A. W., justice of peace

On The Road To Nowhere

Bibliography

Apache-Sitgreaves National Forests. "Recreational Opportunities." USDA, Forest Service, Southwestern Region, 1979.

Arizona Daily Star. Tucson, Arizona, 17 May 1953.

Arizona State Business Directory. Denver: The Gazetteer Publishing & Printing Co.

Avery, Ben. "Spanish Settler Begins Community's Growth." *Arizona Republic.* Phoenix, Arizona, 6 July 1952.

Barnes, Will C. Rev. and enl. by Byrd H. Granger. *Arizona Place Names.* Tucson: The University of Arizona Press, 1960.

Becker Family Collection. Tucson: Arizona Historical Society Library.

Bender, Rod. *Field Guide to Fishing.* Phoenix: Arizona Recreational Publications.

"Blackfeet Man: James Willard Schultz." *Montana Heritage Series,* No. 12. Montana Historical Society, 1961.

Buehler, William J. President: White Mountain Historical Society, Springerville, Arizona. Letter to Karen M. Applewhite, 8 May 1979.

Butler, John. Notes on History of Greer, ca. 1937. Courtesy of Vince Butler, South Fork, Springerville, Arizona.

Butler, Mollie Life Sketch. Phoenix: Department of Library, Archives and Public Records, State Capitol Building.

Butler, Nelson. "Maverick, Arizona." Mimeographed. Courtesy of Southwest Forest Industries. Phoenix, Arizona, 3 May 1978.

Clayton, Roberta. "Pioneer Women of Navajo County." Unpublished Manuscript. Mesa: Arizona Branch, Genealogical Library [LDS].

Crosby, George H. Jr. "As My Memory Recalls: The Hashknife Outfit." *St. Johns Observer.* St. Johns, Arizona, 1 March 1924.

DeWitt, E. R. St. Johns, Arizona. Letter to John Butler. Courtesy of Vince Butler, South Fork, Springerville, Arizona, 15 January 1937.

Dittmar, Victor H. "At 89, Ed Becker Retires—Just a Little." *White Mountain Independent.* Springerville, Arizona, 24 April 1979.

Dyck, Paul. "Lone Wolf Returns." *Montana: The Magazine of Western History.* Winter, 1972.

"Eliza Catherine Rudd Tells of Early History." *White Mountain Roundup.* Springerville, Arizona, 3 July 1970.

"Fatality is Result of Shock." *Arizona Republic.* Phoenix, Arizona, 5 March 1940.

Fitzpatrick, George, and Tucker, Edwin A. *Men Who Matched the Mountains: The Forest Service in the Southwest.* United States Department of Agriculture, Forest Service, Western Division, 1972.

Hale, Sylvester. Eagar, Arizona. Letter to John Butler. n.d. Courtesy of Vince Butler, South Fork, Springerville, Arizona.

Hall, John O. Family Papers. Courtesy of Laverl Hall, St. Johns, Arizona.

Hamblin, John A. *Heritage: A Personal History.* Mesa: Emby Originals, 1977.

Hamblin, Thomas Howell. "Pioneer Tells of Hardships." Newspaper Article. n.d., n.p. Phoenix: Department of Library, Archives and Public Records, State Capitol Building.

Hamilton, Patrick. Arizona Immigration Commissioner in 1884. "Arizona—An Historical Outline." *Arizona Historical Review* (April, 1928).

Haskett, Bert. "Early History of the Cattle Industry in Arizona." *Arizona Historical Review* (October, 1935).

_____. "History of the Sheep Industry in Arizona." *Arizona Historical Review* (July, 1936).

Haws, Atella, Wiltbank, Milo, and Hamblin, Twylah. Compilers. *Eagar Ward, St. Johns Stake: Church of Jesus Christ of Latter Day Saints: Dedicatory Service,* 6 May 1951.

Hinton, Richard J. *The Handbook to Arizona: Its Resources, History, Towns, Mines, Ruins and Scenery.* San Francisco: Payot, Upham & Co., 1878; Reprint Edit., Tucson: Arizona Silhouettes, 1954.

"History of Highways Going to Springerville." *White Mountain Roundup.* Springerville, Arizona, 3 July 1970.

James, George Wharton. *Arizona the Wonderland.* Boston: The Page Co., 1917.

Jenson, Andrew. *Encyclopedic History of the Church of Jesus Christ of Latter-day Saints.* Salt Lake City: Corporation of the President of the Church [LDS], 1941.

Leeds, Dan. Greer, Arizona. Letter to Karen M. Applewhite, 26 March 1979.

Levine, Albert J. *From Indian Trails to Jet Trails.* Snowflake Historical Society, 1977.

"Manuscript History of Greer Ward." Salt Lake City: Archives, LDS Church Historical Department.

Patterson, M. Alice Berry. "Apache County's Immense Wealth of Forest." *Arizona Magazine* (August, 1911).

Pattie, James O. *Personal Narrative of James O. Pattie of Kentucky.* Cincinnati: John H. Wood, 1831: Reprint Edit., Vol. XVIII, *Early Western Travels: 1748-1846,* Ed., Reuben Gold Thwaites, Cleveland: Arthur H. Clark Company, 1905.

Peterson, Charles S. *Take Up Your Mission: Mormon Colonizing Along the Little Colorado River, 1870-1900.* Tucson: The University of Arizona Press, 1973.

Pollock, Paul W. *American Biographical Encyclopedia.* Phoenix: By the Author, 1967. Vol. I.

Reinhold, Ryan. "Mt. Baldy." *White Mountains of Arizona* (1978).

Rhoton, Kent. Navopache Electric Co-Operative, Inc. Lakeside, Arizona. Letter to Karen M. Applewhite, 22 March 1979.

Schultz, James Willard, and Bouldin, Dr. T. J. "A Few Facts About Apache County." St. Johns: St. Johns Observer Printers, 1915.

Schultz, James Willard. *In the Great Apache Forest: The Story of a Lone Boy Scout.* Boston: Houghton Mifflin Company, 1920.

Summerhayes, Martha. *Vanished Arizona: Recollections of My Army Life.* Philadelphia: J. B. Lippincott Company, 1908; Reprint Edit., Philadelphia: J. B. Lippincott Company, 1963.

Udall, Levi S. Arizona Supreme Court Justice. "Gustav Becker, Springerville—Memorial Day Address." Springerville, Arizona, 30 May 1948. Phoenix: Department of Library, Archives and Public Records, State Capitol Building.

Wagoner, Jay. *Arizona's Heritage.* Santa Barbara: Peregrine Smith, Inc., 1977.

White Mountain Independent. Springerville, Arizona, 31 May 1979.

Wilder, Judith Carlock (Mrs. Carleton). Tucson, Arizona. Letter to Karen M. Applewhite, July, 1979.

Williamson, Dan R. "Al Sieber, Famous Scout of the Southwest." *Arizona Historical Review* (January, 1931).

Willson, Roscoe G. "Arizona Days: In Arizona's Hayday." *Arizona Republic.* Phoenix, Arizona, 24 June 1979.

Wiltbank, Effie May Butler Papers. Tucson: Arizona Historical Society Library.

Wiltbank, Milo. "Fireside Memories." Poem. Composed in Greer, Arizona, 1962.

Winn, Fred. "The Apache National Forest." The Fred Winn Collection. Tucson: Arizona Historical Society Library. Mimeographed.

_____. "The Story of Lee Valley and Greer." *Arizona Cattlelog* (July, 1969).

Interviews

Avery Ben. Phoenix, Arizona. Taped interview, 26 February 1979.

Becker, E. C. Springerville, Arizona. Telephone interview, 15 July 1979.

Beer, Paul. Phoenix, Arizona. Taped interview, 28 March 1979.

Butler, Vince. South Fork, Springerville, Arizona. Taped interview, 8 March 1979.

Carlock, G. R. Phoenix, Arizona. Telephone interview, 3 May 1979.

Coggins, Milt Sr. Phoenix, Arizona. Taped interview, 21 April 1979.

Coulter, Dean. Phoenix, Arizona. Taped interview, 28 March 1979.

Crosby, George E., and Florence. Mesa, Arizona. Personal interview, 21 May 1979.

Decker, Katherine Coffin (Mrs. Harold C.). Phoenix, Arizona. Taped interview, 22 February 1979.

Dentzer, Ed G. Jr. Phoenix, Arizona. Taped interview, 26 February 1979.

DeWitt, Willmirth. St. Johns, Arizona. Taped interview, Milo Wiltbank Collection. Tucson: Arizona Historical Society Library, 1957.

Entrekin, Donna (Mrs. Leland). Apache Junction, Arizona. Telephone interview, 27 April 1979.

121

Evans, Denver, and Farris, Barbara Evans. Paradise Valley, Arizona. Personal interview, 2 May 1979.

Gillespie, Mary Ross, M. D. Phoenix, Arizona. Taped interview, 28 March 1979.

Haws, Atella Wiltbank (Mrs. Carl). Eagar, Arizona. Taped interview, 7 March 1979.

Herrod, Julian. Phoenix, Arizona. Taped interview, 31 March 1979.

Jones, Clayton. Phoenix, Arizona. Personal interview, May, 1979.

Leeds, Arthur. Greer, Arizona. Taped interview, 9 March 1979.

Lund, Irl. Eagar, Arizona. Taped interview, 7 March 1979.

Ryley, Fritzie Struckmeyer (Mrs. Francis J.). Phoenix, Arizona. Taped interview, 17 April 1979.

Sharp, Cora Gibbons (Mrs. Clair). Shumway, Arizona. Taped interview, 14 April 1979.

Shields, Charles S. Recreation and Land Staff Officer, Springerville Ranger District, Apache-Sitgreaves National Forest, Springerville, Arizona. Taped interview, 9 March 1979.

Thompson, William B. Pasadena, California. Telephone interview, 16 May 1979.

Wiltbank Afton Haws (Mrs. John Cleveland). Tucson, Arizona. Taped interview, 28 February 1979.

Wiltbank, Mae Hale (Mrs. Milo). Mesa, Arizona. Taped interview, 21 March 1979.

Wolf, Lone (Hart Schultz). Greer, Arizona. Taped interview, Milo Wiltbank Collection. Tucson: Arizona Historical Society Library, ca. 1956.